Berlin Between Two Worlds

About the Book and Editors

Berlin has been a central issue in the postwar dispute between East and West and was often the spark that brought the Soviet bloc and the West to the brink of confrontation. Although the city's role in international politics has been muted in the nearly quarter century since the erection of the Berlin Wall, its political status remains unsettled, and its potential to precipitate a crisis and even a military conflict has lessened only by degree. The contributors to this volume discuss Berlin's future from the perspective of all the major national actors involved. Just as the Quadripartite Agreement of 1971 was a necessary prerequisite for East-West detente, any future change in the division of Germany or in East-West relations will require fundamental shifts in long-held positions on the status of Berlin. The authors show how the perceptions, stakes, and even risks of the Berlin issue vary by nation and explore the reasons why Berlin is likely to continue to be an obstacle to East-West cooperation.

Ronald A. Francisco is associate professor of political science and Soviet and East European studies at the University of Kansas. He is co-editor of *Agricultural Policies in the USSR and Eastern Europe* (Westview, 1980). Richard L. Merritt is professor of political science and research professor of communications at the University of Illinois, Urbana-Champaign. He is co-editor of *Living with the Wall: West Berlin, 1961-1985* (1985).

Published in cooperation with the
Aspen Institute, Berlin, and the
International Institute for Comparative
Social Research, Science Center, Berlin

Berlin Between Two Worlds

edited by Ronald A. Francisco
and Richard L. Merritt

Westview Press / Boulder and London

Westview Special Studies in International Relations

Published in 1986 in the United States of America by Westview Press, Inc.; Frederick A. Praeger, Publisher; 5500 Central Avenue, Boulder, Colorado 80301

Library of Congress Cataloging in Publication Data

Berlin between two worlds
   (Westview special studies in international relations)
   Includes index.
   1. Berlin (Germany)--Politics and government--
Addresses, essays, lectures. 2. World politics--
1945-   --Addresses, essays, lectures. I. Francisco,
Ronald A. II. Merritt, Richard L. III. Series.
DD881.B4663   1986   943.1'55   85-26488
ISBN 0-8133-7131-7

Printed and bound in the United States of America

10 9 8 7 6 5 4 3 2 1

Contents

viii

PART THREE
PROSPECTS FOR BERLIN: ECONOMIC AND SOCIAL TRENDS

Tables and Figures

Foreword

It is now almost a quarter of a century since the Berlin wall was built. Its construction was a watershed in European and, indeed, international politics. It put a seal on Germany's postwar division, made it clear that the Soviet bloc was not prepared to stand by as the German Democratic Republic appeared to fall apart, and demonstrated the Western determination to maintain West Berlin as part of its world. Looked at in another way, however, the wall was one more event in a long series of situations in which East and West learned how to live with one another.

Ever since August 13, 1961, there have been many interpretations of what had happened and predictions of what was to come. The range of such analyses included:

- That the West would not tolerate the wall, that it would insist on its removal as a precondition to any negotiations aimed at stabilizing the political situation in central Europe;
- That the wall symbolized the moral collapse of communism and signaled its eventual bankruptcy as well;
- That sealing off the borders of West Berlin would give the German Democratic Republic the breathing space it needed to develop its own sense of national or at least political identity, which in turn would lead to an easing of living conditions for its citizens;
- That the wall would undermine the political raison d'être of West Berlin and inevitably push the city to the periphery of West German life.

None of these dramatic predictions came true, though each has not been without significance. The West did insist on an amelioration of conditions before signing final agreements with the East, the harshness of Soviet control over Eastern Europe has softened albeit not disappeared, life in the GDR has improved in some respects, and, although West Berlin is not the crisis center it once was, such events as the Berlin elections of 1981 and reception of Ronald W. Reagan thirteen months later indicate that the city's impact is felt throughout the Federal Republic and the West.

Yet the question remains: What difference has the wall made--to Berliners, to Germans, to the rest of the world? This and related problems led the Aspen Institute Berlin and Science Center Berlin, with financial support from the West Berlin Senate, to convene a conference in June 1981 to focus on changes in the city since the construction of the wall.

The participants included policymakers active in setting Allied and West German policy during the crisis of 1961, officials from West Berlin and the Federal Republic, and interested scholars. Two days of the conference looked at the impact of the wall on West Berlin's external political environment. An initial question focused on the situation that surrounds the island-city: What is the German Democratic Republic's policy regarding West Berlin? Although successful in 1961 in gaining Soviet support to build its "wall of peace," the GDR was not able to make good its claim that West Berlin was rightfully part of its own sovereign territory. To what extent is the GDR's strategy still geared to that goal? Is its current tactic of quiet rapprochement with the Federal Republic of Germany simply a new attempt to isolate West Berlin still further? And what role has the Berlin question played in the GDR's relations with its sometimes nervous allies in the Warsaw Pact?

A second question addressed the goals and policies of the Federal Republic. The FRG has faced the dilemma of trying simultaneously to insulate West Berlin against harassment from the East and to integrate the city as fully into its federal system as the Four Powers (and especially its Western allies) permit. To what extent has it been successful in walking the tightrope of such a policy? Has the necessity to maintain West Berlin been more a hindrance in seeking detente in central Europe or an instrument in its relations with the West?

A third kind of question explored at the conference was the place of the Berlin question in the relationship of the four wartime Allies, first, with each other and, second, with their client-states in Germany. A continuation of Four-Power agreements gives the United States, Great Britain, France, and the Soviet Union responsibilities and privileges in Germany and Europe as a whole; and this relationship in turn impinges on the linkages these countries have with their other allies in the region. How have the Powers balanced the costs of the Berlin situation with the leverage it provides? In what circumstances might they be willing to promote or accept a significant change in West Berlin's status?

This volume presents the papers (updated in summer 1985) on West Berlin's external relations delivered at the conference. A second volume, <u>Living with the Wall:</u> <u>West Berlin, 1961-1985</u>, edited by Richard L. and Anna J. Merritt (Durham, North Carolina: Duke University Press, 1985) contains the papers presented during the first two days of the conference, which dealt with the effect on West Berlin itself of the wall and Quadripartite Agreement. Together, the two volumes provide a comprehensive picture of what has been--and in many ways remains--one of the world's most fascinating cities, Berlin.

Shepard Stone

1

Introduction: Divided Berlin in Postwar Politics

Ronald A. Francisco

Berlin has been a central issue in the postwar dispute between East and West. Often it has been the site of political tensions that brought the Soviet bloc and the West to the brink of open combat. Its geographic location, unique political status, and dramatic division have made Berlin an important symbol in the struggle for the control of Germany and central Europe. Berlin's present role in international politics is noticeably muted. Yet its political status remains essentially unchanged. It remains sharply divided between East and West even after the past decade's concessions from both sides. Its geographic locations is now no less important strategically or politically.

The Berlin of the 1980s owes its relative quiescence to the diplomacy of the 1970s. By the late 1960s most of the relevant national actors had sufficient incentive to work to defuse the tension that had grown out of the conflicts and raw politics of the previous two decades. Yet because Berlin's political status remains unsettled, its potential to precipitate a crisis and even a military conflict has lessened only by degree. Berlin's future lies in the hands of a diverse set of actors that operates on three basic levels: East versus West; East Germany versus West Germany; and to a lesser extent East Berlin versus West Berlin. The combinations and permutations that occur within and between these levels have become increasingly complex, and are reflected in the multiplicity of international perspectives represented in this volume.

This introduction explores Berlin's international position by reviewing the major events of the postwar era in the context of the foreign policy perspective of the major actors. As the subsequent chapters show, the motives and goals of these actors have varied widely and often conflicted directly throughout the postwar period. In fact, much of the intensity of the Berlin problem can be traced to the fact that its postwar structure was jointly designed by allies who failed to anticipate the fundamental political struggle that was to grip Europe

2

in the wake of World War II.

POSTWAR ARRANGEMENTS AND THE ONSET OF CONFLICT

Planning for the postwar occupation of Germany began as soon as the war turned in the Allies' favor. The foreign ministers of the United Kingdom, United States, and Soviet Union met in Moscow in autumn 1943. They established an apparatus, the European Advisory Commission, to devise a common strategy based on the principle of joint occupation of Germany. Within a year the European Advisory Commission had established prospective occupation boundaries and agreed to a separate, joint occupation of Berlin. In November 1944 an Allied Control Council was proposed to coordinate the policies of all zones and sectors of occupation in Germany and Berlin.

The agreements were ratified in early 1945 by the three powers at Yalta, where France was added as an occupying power. Planning was thus quite complete when the Red Army succeeded in its conquest of Berlin in May, and when Germany surrendered formally a week later. In June American, British, French, and Soviet military commanders signed the Berlin agreement, formalizing their supreme authority in Germany. British and American forces arrived in Berlin in July and the formal sectoral occupation of Berlin commenced.

The centrifugal force inherent in a structure of four separate national occupation zones certainly carried the seeds of conflict in Berlin. But this situation was exacerbated by events beyond the city, and even beyond Germany. Berlin became a kind of crucible of East-West conflict. As local political and administrative issues began to reveal recognizable differences between the Soviet Union and the Western powers, matters were worsening elsewhere. The United States and United Kingdom had differed sharply with the USSR at the Potsdam conference over the amount of German reparations and the Soviet role in Eastern Europe. When the USSR refused to vacate the northern provinces of Iran after the war, the Western allies forced action in the United Nations. The USSR sided openly with the communist forces in the Greek civil war. The United States responded directly with the Truman doctrine. Meanwhile, the Soviet Union's policies in its zone of occupation outside Berlin stirred concern among the Western allies.

All of these problems had an indirect but cumulative effect in Berlin. Berlin was one of three instances of common governance in the world where the principal actors of the two emerging ideological blocs

not only met directly, but also forged <u>common</u> policy.1/
The Soviet Union devoted considerable energies to the
political reorganization in its own mold and consolidation of its zones of occupation. It sought nonetheless to retain the quadripartite character of Berlin and
allowed the first scheduled postwar municipal elections
(in October 1946) to proceed in the Soviet sector.

The Soviet entry in the election was the newly
organized Socialist Unity party (SED, Sozalistische
Einheitspartei Deutschlands). The party was the product
of a forced (and eventually incomplete) merger of the
revamped Social Democratic and Communist parties.<u>2</u>/ The
election was a rare instance in which the USSR took the
political risk of open public rejection in an area under
its military control. The Soviet-backed SED lost badly,
even in (Soviet-controlled) East Berlin. It was clear
that the Soviets would now need to intensify their
political authority in East Berlin in order to achieve
the sort of monolithic political hierarchy they were
building elsewhere in Eastern Europe.

The focus of East-West conflict shifted away from
Berlin following the municipal elections. This was a
period of generally poor relations, with major
disagreements appearing over Greece and continuing
Soviet policies in Eastern Europe. Most relevant for
Berlin, however, was the Anglo-American economic merger
of occupation zones in December 1946. Soviet
intransigence in Four-power talks had convinced the
United States and United Kingdom that genuine
quadripartite administration of Germany was incompatible
with economic progress and political development.

The year 1948 brought a new nadir in East-West
relations. Early in February a communist coup seized
power in Prague and transformed Czechoslovakia into a

---

1. The city of Vienna was also jointly occupied, but
central command was rotated monthly among the Allies.
The United States, United Kingdom, and France shared
seats with the USSR on the United Nations Security
Council, but this was not generally an instance of
mandatory common policy making. In the strict sense,
then, Berlin's was the only situation in the world that
demanded constant coordinated decisionmaking between
East and West.

2. The Social Democratic party (SPD) leaders in West
Germany and Berlin protested the merger. The Four-power
status of Berlin permitted the perpetuation of an SPD
branch until it was dissolved for the protection of its
membership in 1961. See Richard L. Merritt and Ronald
A. Francisco, "The SPD of East Berlin, 1945-1961,"
<u>Comparative Politics</u> 5:1 (October 1972): 1-29.

Soviet satellite. American Marshall Plan aid was spurned by the USSR, which also forbade its Eastern European allies to accept any American funds. The growing "cold war" had intensified and soon settled with a vengeance on Berlin.

In March 1948 the Soviet military administration began to restrict traffic between Western occupation zones and Berlin. These restrictions grew throughout the spring. They represented the Soviets' response to rapidly developing efforts in the Western zones to establish a separate, integrated economic and administrative system. The Soviets had already done much in their own zone to organize an independent, Soviet-style political and economic order. Nonetheless, the USSR protested Western policies vigorously and then went so far as to merge the East Berlin police force with the forces of the Soviet occupation zone (a violation of Berlin's separate, Four-power status).

Ignoring Soviet protests, the three Western powers allowed control of economic policy to revert to German civilian authorities and sanctioned a currency reform that effectively separated the economies of the Western zones from the Soviet zone and Berlin. The USSR responded five days later with its own currency reform, designed for its occupation zone and all of Berlin (citing Berlin as an integral part of the East German economy). The Western commandants in Berlin ruled the Soviet order invalid for their sectors and protested against the sudden severance of electrical service to West Berlin. The following day West German currency was introduced in West Berlin. The two parts of the city now operated under separate currencies and economic systems. The formal division of Berlin was under way.

In response, the Soviets intensified their efforts to isolate West Berlin. Their blockade of land routes from West Germany was made nearly absolute. Land vehicles were prevented from leaving West Germany for Berlin. Stalin apparently felt that the risk of military conflict was outweighed by the potential gains from a direct challenge to the Western position in Berlin and Germany. The blockade was, according to Philip Windsor, "a substitute for war" from the Soviet perspective.3/

It is doubtful that Stalin had ever envisioned the West's bold and ingenious response: the Berlin Airlift. U.S. General Lucius D. Clay persuaded a skeptical group of superiors in both Washington and Britain that West Berlin could be supplied by air alone, given feasible additions to the available fleet of aircraft and

---

3. Philip Windsor, <u>City on Leave: A History of Berlin, 1945-1962</u> (London: Chatto and Windus, 1963), p. 98.

improvement of Berlin's airports. For eleven months airplanes landed in Berlin every five minutes, ferrying the city's every needed resource, albeit never in completely sufficient quantities. It was a magnificent technical achievement and the Berliners united behind it with tremendous zeal.

The political embarrassment of the successful airlift and the growing effect of an Allied counterblockade against the Soviet zone led Stalin to resume negotiations and finally to lift the blockade. Yet the end of the blockade of Berlin was in no sense a return to normalcy. Germany and Berlin were now resolutely divided between East and West. West Berlin became a separate political unit, with Ernst Reuter as its first governing mayor. By the end of 1949 constitutions had been promulgated in both East and West Germany and new republics were proclaimed--two separate German states.

With the establishment of the Federal Republic of Germany (FRG) in the West and the German Democratic Republic (GDR) in the East, one of the fundamental postwar political struggles ended its first phase. For Berlin it was a time of great insecurity. The Western powers had forbidden the inclusion of West Berlin in the political competence of the new Federal Republic of Germany. Similarly, East Berlin was to remain, at least formally, separate from the German Democratic Republic. Berlin was to continue to be subject to the authority of the four occupying Powers.

With these developments the international picture became even more complicated. Already the cast of relevant actors was large. But now four new political units emerged and began to interact on the question of Berlin. These were, of course, the two new German republics and the two separate governments of Berlin. The network of relationships that formed around the Berlin question was clearly delineated between East and West, with very little communication or cooperation between actors at most levels. Even the interaction of East and West Berlin occurred mostly along functional lines, for example, some municipal services.

While the Soviet Union continued to consolidate its political control in the East, things were considerably different in the West. Berlin's new mayor found communication easier with the Powers that ruled his city than with the West German leadership in Bonn.4/ This was a problem that was to persist throughout the long tenure of Chancellor Konrad Adenauer. It arose not only because of the Federal Republic's lack of legal authority over West Berlin, but also because of

---

4. See ibid., pp. 131-135.

6

Adenauer's own views.

Adenauer was already an old man whose perceptions
had been shaped with considerable definition by his
environment and experiences. He had fought in his
political youth against both the Prussian Protestant
Junkers and the anti-clerical Social Democrats from
Berlin. As Lewis Edinger points out:

> He came to dislike both the "blue" and the "red"
> Prussians intensely, and he felt a far closer af-
> finity with his coreligionists in Western and
> Southern Latin Europe than with his compatriots
> across the Elbe. The world of Berlin and East
> Germany . . . was alien to him--an outpost of
> Western civilization in a Slavic world shaped by
> Byzantine and Asian despots . . . It was from the
> East, rather than the West that the war clouds
> seemed to come when the war broke out in 1914."5/

The fact that Reuter was not only a Berliner, but a
Social Democrat, made matters worse. Adenauer's
subsequent apathy toward Berlin was a problem for
successive governing mayors. It necessitated greater
reliance on the occupying Powers and propelled West
Berlin's political leaders toward a disproportionately
prominent international role.

BERLIN AS A SYMBOL IN THE COLD WAR

The stalwart resistance of the Berlin population
during the blockade focused a great deal of attention on
the city and raised the stakes in the continuing East-
West struggle. As Soviet and East German harassment of
travel and utility services persisted throughout the
1950s, the Western Powers steadfastly maintained their
rights in Berlin. Berlin emerged in the cold war
rhetoric as a beacon of freedom in the darkness beyond
the iron curtain. A major factor in the perpetuation of
this view and the public attention directed at Berlin in
the West was the continuing flow of refugees from the
East.

The refugee flow into West Berlin ebbed and flowed
but never stopped. There is little question that the
massive numbers of East Germans and East Berliners who
fled to the West had mixed motives. While they were
seen in the West principally as political refugees, many
certainly were driven to leave by the grinding poverty

---

5. Lewis J. Edinger, _Kurt Schumacher: A Study in
Personality and Political Behavior_ (Stanford, CA: Stanford University Press, 1965), pp. 215-216.

in East Germany (where food rationing, for example, continued until 1958). The East Berlin and East German economy still suffered the effects of the USSR's reparation policy, which involved the dismantling and removal of industrial plants. The Soviet Union's insistence that the GDR accept no Marshall Plan funds meant that the critical investment capital that flowed into the West was denied to the East. The GDR's position was eroded also by the flow of refugees itself. Because working-age, better educated, and skilled people were more likely to emigrate, the GDR had difficulty maintaining professional staffs and skilled construction crews. Other jobs were scarce. Many East Berliners became Grenzgaenger--those who crossed the border to work in West Berlin. Clearly, the transition to socialism was going badly.

The situation had not improved by the time Stalin died in March 1953. The change in Soviet leadership brought hope for a breakthrough on the status of Berlin. Ernst Reuter was convinced that this was a propitious moment for the settlement of the whole Berlin question.6/ Optimism in the West rose not only from Stalin's death, but because the Soviets showed serious concern over Western ideas about an active West European military alliance against the Soviet Union. The proposed European Defense Community was to be a common European force to supplement American guarantees under the NATO treaty. The principal issue of controversy--in the West as well as in the East--was the inclusion of West Germany in these efforts. The United States had pressed for rearmament of the Federal Republic since the outbreak of the Korean War. The new Soviet leadership now entered in the midst of Western preparations for the EDC and German rearmament.

There is no assurance that the USSR seriously intended at this point to do what its vague diplomacy implied: Reunite Germany as a neutral, disarmed buffer nation. Nonetheless, many Europeans, including Reuter, pressed Western leaders to sound out the Soviet proposals. Before much progress had been made, however, the continuing economic problems in the GDR led to a workers' uprising on June 17, 1953. The rebellion, initially a protest against a drastic increase in production norms, soon expanded to a political challenge to the GDR regime itself. It was brutally supressed by East German police backed up by Soviet tanks. The anniversary of the uprising in 1953 is commemorated in West Germany as the "Day of German Unity." The irony, however, is that the explosive force and rapid escalation of the uprising convinced Soviet authorities that

---

6. Windsor, <u>City on Leave</u>, p. 152.

still tighter controls were necessary. The settlement of the German problem would have to wait.7/

The uprising in 1953 again turned the eyes of the world to Berlin, but events soon shifted the spotlight back to the attempt of the West to forge a credible, integrated military alliance while the Soviet Union applied countervailing pressure. After Ernst Reuter died suddenly in the fall of 1953, Adenauer again stood out in the wooing from East and West that has been West Germany's particular experience during much of the postwar era. There was little question where Adenauer stood. Above all, and for various reasons, he sought an alliance of the West against the threat of the Soviet Union. He stressed this consistently. Berlin was of course a concern, but one that would be solved only in the context of a strong Western alliance and a freely reunified Germany.

The issue of German rearmament within the context of West Europe and, eventually, NATO overshadowed efforts in 1954 and 1955 to conclude a German settlement among the four Powers. The Soviets exerted tremendous pressure to dissuade West Europe from approving the EDC and rearming Germany. They won an unexpected and shortlived victory in 1954 when the French National Assembly refused to approve the EDC, largely because of misgivings over German rearmament. The United States and United Kingdom responded quickly, however, and within a year a new plan to integrate West German military forces into an upgraded North Atlantic Treaty Organization had won approval by the French.

The USSR was diligent in the period before the final ratification of the new NATO agreements. It warned on one hand that any such alliance, particularly one including West Germany, would oblige it to form its own counterpart. An alliance also would perpetuate the division of Germany. On the other hand, in 1955 the Soviets offered substantial verbal commitments to reunified Germany with free elections.8/ During the year, they took tangible steps to increase their credibility. The Soviets withdrew from Finland, Austria, and Port Arthur.9/ They made unparalleled concession on nuclear disarmament in bilateral negotiations with the United States.10/ Even after the NATO

---

7. See ibid., pp. 153-158.

8. See ibid., p. 187.

9. David J. Dallin, <u>Soviet Foreign Policy after Stalin</u> (Philadelphia: Lippincott, 1961), p. 261.

10. See Lloyd Jensen, "Soviet-American Bargaining

treaties were approved by the German Bundestag in May 1955, the Soviets maintained their diplomatic offensive. They matched the West's every move (giving sovereignty to the GDR just four months after the Federal Republic's own sovereignty and continuing efforts to build the Soviet bloc's equivalent to NATO--the Warsaw Pact). Yet at the same time they maintained their commitment to a new European security arrangement that might obviate NATO, the Warsaw Pact, and German rearmament.

The West's rejection of the Soviet proposals led to a shift in the USSR's position. By the end of 1955 it sought some sort of ratification of the status quo-- including a divided Germany and Berlin. The Soviet invited Chancellor Adenauer to Moscow. He accepted, and in December 1955, to the displeasure of the United States, exchanged diplomatic recognition with the Soviet Union. Adenauer had, in effect, ratified the division of Germany and the continuing insecurity of Berlin.11/

Events in the ensuing years were to intensify the division of Europe, Germany, and Berlin. This was particularly difficult for Berlin. It meant not only practical and physical hardship, but increased prospects for long-term isolation and separation. The mutual actions of leaders in the East and West in 1955 had divided Germany into two sovereign states without solving the problem of divided Berlin. Berlin's real hope, perhaps only feasible hope, had been a general settlement that might have linked both East and West Germany with Berlin as a central or capital city, or at minimum clearly defined legal and political ties between the FRG and West Berlin.

Berlin as Lever and Obstacle

Once Berlin was omitted from an overalll political settlement in Germany, its status in the East-West struggle began to shift subtly. On the one hand, the Western powers continued steadfastly to support and defend their rights in the city, but this had to be done in the face of increasing Soviet pressure and capability. In addition, it now appeared that Berlin's status would require very long-term political and military support from the United States, France, and the United Kingdom. Plainly there would be periods in which the defense of Berlin might conflict with these nations' other goals and interests. Nor could conflict among the

---

Behavior in the Postwar Disarmament Negotiations," _Journal of Conflict Resolution_ 7 (1963): 522-541.

11. See Windsor, _City on Leave_, pp. 191-195.

Allies be precluded. On the other hand, the Soviet Union had to put up with the continued existence of an island of capitalism and Western propaganda in the midst of its most critical front-line ally. Khrushchev often remarked that West Berlin was a "bone in the throat" or a "cancerous tumor."12/

West Berlin was in fact a distinct irritant for the USSR and even more intensely for the GDR. First, it was a relatively open outlet for emigration, and refugees flowed through each month by the thousands. Second, Berlin's geographic location, closer to Poland than to the Federal Republic, meant that its strong radio (and later television) transmissions could reach large areas of the GDR otherwise inaccessible to West German transmitters. Third, it provided Western military and intelligence access at a point behind the Warsaw Pact's frontline.

By 1958 two new individuals had solidified their positions in the international wrangling over Berlin. The first was Willy Brandt, who became governing mayor of West Berlin in October 1957. The second was Nikita Khrushchev. He had emerged from the lengthy succession battles in Moscow as the unchallenged leader. Ironically, both of these figures owed a measure of their new political power to their roles in the Soviet suppression of the Hungarian revolt--Khrushchev for its success, Brandt for his ability to restrain West Berliners from charging into East Berlin to protest it. The Soviet action in Hungary had been an important event. It showed the continuing instability of Eastern Europe and resolve of the USSR, and also demonstrated the limits of Western resolve. The Soviets had exploited internal Western disputes over Suez to launch a major test of the United States' massive retaliation doctrine in Europe. The West's failure to respond directly gave a significant signal to the Soviets.

By 1958 Khrushchev felt strong enough to issue a direct challenge to the West in its most vulnerable spot: Berlin. The Soviets clearly perceived Berlin as an excellent lever to test the will of the Western alliance and to challenge its basic posture regarding Germany. Adam Ulam points out also that the timing of the Soviet action in 1958 "leaves no doubt as to the wider context in which the Soviets made their move"--the Sino-Soviet dispute was beginning, and Khrushchev needed a ringing success in Europe. What better place to gain it than in Berlin?13/

---

12. Arthur M. Schlesinger, Jr., A Thousand Days (Boston: Houghton Mifflin, 1965), p. 345.

13. Adam B. Ulam, Expansion and Coexistence, 2nd ed.

On November 27, 1958 Soviet ambassadors in the capitals of the Western powers delivered diplomatic notes to the respective heads of government. The communication was a lengthy Soviet demand for a normalization of the situation in Berlin--on Soviet terms. Berlin was to become a free city, the Allies were to leave, and all this was to happen within six months. The alternative was a vague threat to turn over control of the situation to the GDR (presumably after a separate peace treaty) which could then deal with access to Berlin as an independent, sovereign state. The Western powers refused to negotiate under this form of direct threat. A second Soviet note in January 1959 was more explicit. The USSR directly threatened to sign a separate peace treaty with the GDR.

Alarmed, British Prime Minister Macmillan set off for a visit with Khrushchev in Moscow. The two seem to have come to some sort of consensus about the need for a general settlement in Germany. Soviet rhetoric eased, and the six-month time period of the ultimatum was extended. Macmillan found poor response to his plan in the West, however, especially in West Germany. Adenauer wanted no part of a deal between the Western powers and the Soviets that would compromise the status of the Federal Republic and its full ties to the West.

The foreign ministers of the four Powers met in Geneva from May until August, with no result. At a minimum, though, the deadline of the ultimatum had passed without incident, and the Soviets seemed less insistent on Western compliance with a firm date. In fact, in September 1959, in summit talks with President Eisenhower at Camp David, Khrushchev apparently dropped the Soviet demand for a firm deadline. The status of Berlin remained unchanged.

Khrushchev had failed to win his clear victory, but the West had little to celebrate. As Philip Windsor points out:

> The morale of the Berlin population had been great-
> ly shaken, the irresolution of the Western gov-
> ernments before the remotest prospect of nuclear
> war had been exposed, and it had been demonstrated
> that . . . they were unable to devise any alter-
> natives to the status quo. They had shown that
> they did not consider it feasible to hold Berlin
> indefinitely against Soviet pressure and . . .
> [were] unwilling to resist petty acts of provoca-
> tion on the part of the East German regime.14/

(New York: Praeger, 1974), p. 619.

14. Windsor, *City on Leave*, p. 219.

The Berlin that had withstood the blockade and been the symbol of the will of the West emerged from the second postwar Berlin crisis appearing much more vulnerable and less a symbol now than an obstacle to Western unity and to accommodation with the USSR in Europe.

The Wall

The government of the GDR apparently decided in 1960 to force some sort of settlement that would ameliorate at least the worst consequence that West Berlin represented: the refugee problem. Yet, to force a solution, it had to convince the Soviet Union that a radical policy (such as sealing the border between East and West Berlin) would produce net benefits that would outweigh the risks of direct conflict with the West. The GDR thus began to adopt policies that exacerbated the refugee flow. It announced the prospective collectivization of agriculture, tightened the economic system, and did not effectively discourage speculation that the border was about to be sealed. The result was a flood of refugees that all but overwhelmed facilities in West Berlin and West Germany.

Meanwhile, talks among the four Powers had broken down with the failure of the Paris Conference in May 1960. The United States was in the midst of an election campaign. The Soviet Union had failed to wrest from the West acquiescence to the notion of West Berlin as a Free City, but neither had it directly endangered the East Berlin regime of Walter Ulbricht by agreeing to some sort of German reunification or confederation. Ulbricht stepped up the pressure. He sought to create conditions that threatened to endanger his regime. This was a risky strategy to be sure, but it was the sort of brinksmanship that would be necessary to gain Soviet approval for a solution to the refugee problem.15/

West Berlin constituted a portal to the West that was unique in the Soviet bloc. No other regime endured what the GDR was forced to tolerate from its founding until 1961. During this period, more than three million refugees emigrated to the West. This amounted to almost 20 per cent of the GDR's entire population. Typically these were the most productive or potentially productive

---

15. See Richard L. Merritt, "A Transformed Crisis: The Berlin Wall," in Living With the Wall: West Berlin, 1961-1985, eds. Richard L. Merritt and Anna J. Merritt (Durham, NC: Duke University Press, 1985), pp. 3-36; Windsor, City on Leave, pp. 220-243.

people.16/
     The flow of refugees remained at a very high level
throughout 1960 and in the first months of 1961.
Ulbricht tried and failed to win support for his plans
from a special Warsaw Pact Council meeting in March.
Sympathy for the plight of the GDR, whatever it was, was
overshadowed by the risks of war with the West and the
embarrassment of building a wall to hold citizens in a
socialist nation. In June President Kennedy and Chair-
man Khrushchev met for summit conference in Vienna.
Both sides restated their previous positions.
Khrushchev repeated the demands of the ultimatum of
1958, and Kennedy stressed the West's insistence on its
continued presence in West Berlin, unrestricted access
to West Berlin, and freedom for West Berliners to determine their own form of government. Kennedy thus
signaled that his administration limited its fundamental
concern to the western sectors of the city. Khrushchev,
in turn, again threatened to sign a separate peace
treaty with the GDR, and sought to underscore his
perception of the danger of war: "Berlin is the most
dangerous spot in the world."17/
     The ensuing month brought increased pressure in the
East and Allied confusion in the West. GDR citizens
fled in increasing, alarming numbers. The situation in
the GDR was deteriorating rapidly, and Ulbricht's
regime did in fact face considerable dangers if nothing
were done. The strange GDR policy left the West
nonplussed. Kennedy and Macmillan had met in June
following the Vienna summit and agreed about basic
approaches. There were differences with France,
however, and Western solidarity was likely to decline as
any Berlin conflict escalated toward war with the
USSR.18/ United States Secretary of State Dean Rusk went
to Paris in August to work out a strategy for negotiations between the Western powers and the Soviet Union.
Objections, principally from the French and West

---

16. In recent years the GDR has been much more forthcoming about the circumstances that led to the Berlin
wall. For example, Heinz Heitzer recently wrote: "The
GDR had kept its border with West Berlin open for years,
although this had resulted in considerable aggravation
as far as socialist construction was concerned. It had
done this in order not to complicate matters with the
FRG and West Berlin." GDR: An Historical Outline (Dres-
den: Verlag Zeit im Bild, 1981), pp. 125-126.

17. Schlesinger, A Thousand Days, p. 371.

18. Ibid., pp. 375-377.

14

Germans, precluded a positive outcome.19/

At this point, however, the die was already cast. With the United States unable to bring its allies together in a common approach, prominent Americans began to signal publicly Kennedy's private position: That Khrushchev would have to do something to stabilize the internal situation, and that, if he did, the West could do little.20/ Khrushchev called a special meeting of the Warsaw Pact Council for August 3. Ulbricht's case, now bolstered by the increased threat to his regime and American signals of acceptance of a sealed border, persuaded the delegates. The decision was announced ten days later as the border was closed and the construction of the wall began.

Reaction in Berlin, predictably, was sharp. On the international and even national level, however, reactions were muted. The United States publicly assured everyone that it did not perceive its interests in Berlin to have been affected, although the Soviets had clearly violated the provisions of the Potsdam agreement. France and the United Kingdom did nothing. In the Federal Republic Willy Brandt was campaigning against Adenauer in national elections. Brandt, although the SPD's candidate for the chancellorship, remained governing mayor of Berlin. He rushed back to the embattled city. Adenauer, however, paid virtually no attention to the Berlin crisis and continued campaigning (even more fiercely) against Brandt.21/

Brandt was outraged by the callous response in the Federal Republic and the feeble inaction of the Western allies. He tried desperately to rally some concerted response. It came only very slowly, however. The Allies did not wish to act rashly in a very explosive situation. In time, measures were taken that indicated the West's indignation over the GDR's and USSR's actions. Military strength in Berlin was increased and Kennedy dispatched both Vice President Johnson and the hero of the Berlin airlift, Lucius Clay, to Berlin. In the meantime the pressure from the East continued. The GDR's official rationale for the wall was issued and remains unchanged:

> The security measures of 13 August 1961 were a joint political action of the Warsaw Treaty states which restrained the aggressive imperialist forces in the FRG and in other NATO countries and saved

---

19. Ibid., pp. 393-394.

20. Ibid., p. 394.

21. See Merritt, "A Transformed Crisis."

peace in Europe.<u>22</u>/

The Soviet Union kept up a diplomatic offensive in the form of a series of diplomatic notes that (obliquely) threatened Western access to Berlin through the air corridors and announced the resumption of Soviet nuclear atmospheric testing.<u>23</u>/
    While the Berliners were shocked at apparent Western indifference, or impotence, the West was relieved. The Soviets and the GDR had taken a minimum step. They had halted the massive egress from the GDR with a concrete wall. Yet they stopped at this. Western military presence remained. West Berlin continued to be a source of destabilizing Western propaganda.<u>24</u>/   Khrushchev, in speaking in October to the Communist Party of the Soviet Union, indicated a willingness to negotiate on Berlin. This, to the Americans at least, signified the end of the 1961 Berlin crisis.<u>25</u>/
    The wall in Berlin chilled East-West relations, but at the same time established a new fundamental basis on which to operate. The Soviet Union had taken the notion of its "sphere of influence" in Eastern Europe one step farther. The East Germans had achieved the minimum policy that would allow them to begin serious work toward economic reconstruction and social consolidation. As Gebhard Schweigler argues: "The wall in Berlin symbolized rather concretely the attempt by the SED to gain that external and internal freedom of maneuver required for a successful development of its own state."<u>26</u>/
    All of this left West Berlin a bit more isolated and insecure. Periodic high-level visits from American leaders (Robert Kennedy in 1962 and President Kennedy himself in 1963) helped to raise morale, but did little for the objective situation in Berlin. Nor were Berliners any more pleased than Konrad Adenauer at the continuing conflicts within the Western alliance, and in

---

22. Heitzer, <u>GDR: An Historical Outline</u>, p. 127.

23. Schlesinger, <u>A Thousand Days</u>, p. 198.

24. Ibid., p. 397.

25. Ibid., p. 400.

26. Gebhard Schweigler, "Whatever Happened to Germany?" in <u>The Foreign Policy of West Germany</u>, eds. E. Krippendorff and V. Rittberger (Beverly Hills, CA: Sage, 1980), p. 106.

particular between France and the United States.<u>27</u>/

CONSOLIDATION AND DETENTE

<u>The Beginnings of Detente</u>

The world paid much less heed to Berlin in the years following the Berlin wall. The immediate crisis had abated, and continuing Eastern harassment of travel rights and access to East Berlin did not resurrect the crisis atmosphere. The attention of the United States and even the Soviet Union was directed elsewhere. Most of the Berlin issues in these years had a local flavor, e.g., efforts to secure for West Berliners access to East Berlin on holidays. Yet the international status of Berlin remained unsettled. The USSR and GDR continued to use diplomatic pressure to isolate West Berlin from West Germany (e.g., in 1964 referring to West Berlin in a treaty as an "independent political entity"). Most important, however, was how fundamentally the wall through and around Berlin had changed the situation in the GDR. The persistent threat to Ulbricht's regime had been brutally but effectively eliminated. GDR citizens, with dim prospects for emigration, began to build the stable economic basis that the GDR had always lacked. The GDR economy proved to be remarkably responsive. Even Western observers spoke of an Eastern "economic miracle" of the 1960s that rivaled West Germany's astonishing growth in the 1950s.

Leaders in the GDR apparently understood the importance of economic performance in the achievement of political legitimacy. Improving the standard of living was a primary policy goal.<u>28</u>/   At least one Western leader comprehended this and sought to capitalize on it. As early as 1963 Willy Brandt had conceived an integrated Western aid program, similar to the Marshall Plan, as key to prospective detente with the East.<u>29</u>/ Brandt,

---

27. See Konrad Adenauer, <u>Erinnerungen, 1959-1963</u> (Stuttgart: Deutsche Verlags Anstalt, 1968), pp. 121-122.

28. See Michael J. Sodaro, "External Influences on Regime Stability in the GDR: A Linkage Analysis," in <u>Foreign and Domestic Policy in Eastern Europe in the 1980s</u>, eds. M.J. Sodaro and S.L. Wolchik (New York: St. Martin's, 1983), pp. 83-85.

29. Arnulf Baring,   <u>Machtwechsel: Die Aera Brandt-Scheel</u> (Stuttgart: Deutsche Verlags Anstalt, 1982), p. 207.

still the city's governing mayor, had a sound understanding of the situation based on personal experience
and intrinsic interest in the welfare of Berliners. His
party, the opposition SPD, maintained secret contacts
with the GDR from 1964 until 1967, although it failed to
win any breakthrough.30/ The GDR had won its sealed
border and was now in no way predisposed to make concessions that would improve the lot of West Berlin.

It was, then, the Soviet Union that played the
critical Eastern role during this period. Moscow's view
of the world had been altered by developments in the
early 1960s. The Berlin wall had been an embarrassing,
if necessary, concession to Walter Ulbricht. 1962
brought the humiliation of the Cuban missile crisis.
The years that followed saw the ouster of Khrushchev,
revealed the ferocity of the Sino-Soviet split, and
hinted strongly of declining East European loyalty.31/
This is not to suggest that the USSR was desperate. For
one thing, the United States was preoccupied with its
own problems in NATO and of course in Vietnam. Even so,
the USSR began to see the benefit of guarded cooperation
in Europe. Detente would co-opt some of the centrifugal
tendencies in Eastern Europe, allow an interval of safety while the USSR built up its military strength, and
might bring economic benefits.32/

Thus the two actors entering the latter half of the
decade with greatest incentive for a relaxation of tension and cooperation in Europe were the USSR and West
Germany (particularly the SPD). The barriers to any
such accommodation, however, were formidable. On the
one hand, the USSR faced the bitter intransigence of the
Ulbricht regime in any scheme to settle the principal
questions surrounding Berlin. Yet such a settlement was
a formal prerequisite for the West. The West Germans,
on the other hand, needed the cooperation of the Western
powers, which required that there be no challenge to the
basic structure of authority in Berlin. Bonn's primary
goal, to establish firmly articulated links between the
FRG and West Berlin, was accordingly subordinated. The
West Germans also had to contend with American skepti-
cism about any accommodation with the East.33/

Berlin stood as the principal obstacle even in the

---

30. See ibid., pp. 213-223.

31. See Philip Windsor, _Germany and the Management of
Detente_ (New York: Praeger, 1971), pp. 11-26.

32. See ibid.; and Baring, _Machtwechsel_, pp. 229-244.

33. See ibid., pp. 262, 277; and Henry Kissinger, _White
House Years_ (Boston: Little, Brown, 1979), p. 409.

tentative first stages of detente. The GDR feared any increased legitimacy for West Berlin. The West Germans refused to sign a peace treaty with the Soviet Union without first receiving a firm commitment to an acceptable interim settlement of the Berlin problem. Philip Windsor has likened the Western conception of structure of detente to a series of concentric circles, with the German question in the center circle and Berlin as its nucleus. Without a settlement of the core issues, there could be no general relaxation of tensions.34/ By contrast, the East sought a basic ratification of the status quo--especially the division of Germany and the legal separation of West Germany and West Berlin.

During the mid-1960s efforts to manage East-West detente at the alliance level proved unwieldy and were abandoned. The basic issues raised controversies within, as well as between alliances.35/ The Soviet-led suppression of the Czechoslovakian reform movement in 1968 is a case in point. Less well known was the GDR's bitter struggled within the Warsaw Pact from 1966 until 1968 for its own "Hallstein doctrine," i.e., "insisting that no socialist country should open diplomatic relations with the Federal Republic until Bonn was ready to recognize East Germany, to accept the existing borders in Europe, . . . and to recognize West Berlin as a separate political unit."36/ Yet the Warsaw Pact refused in 1967 to endorse the policy for the alliance as a whole. Detente was thereafter, both in the East and in the West, pursued inductively--first in the form of bilateral arrangements or specific issue agreements, then in the more general form of East-West treaties such as the Quadripartite Agreement on Berlin and the Helsinki Accords.

Ostpolitik and the Quadripartite Agreement

Philip Windsor completed his excellent history of Berlin not too many months after the construction of the wall.37/ He attempted at the close of the volume to look beyond the anger and pessimism of the moment and to define how the Berlin problem might someday be settled.

----

34. Windsor, Germany and the Management of Detente, p. 30.

35. See ibid., p. 31.

36. Wolfram F. Hanrieder, The Stable Crisis (New York: Harper and Row, 1970), p. 115.

37. Windsor, City on Leave.

He concluded that two essential conditions would have to
be met. First, the USSR "would have to admit West
Germany to some share in the future of Berlin, and West
Germany will have to come to terms, on this question at
least, with the GDR." Second, " . . . The West will
have to come to terms with an eventual recognition of
East Germany."38/ Seen either as prescience or as common sense, Windsor's conditions are remarkable for the
accuracy that they came to represent and for the fact
that even these conditions did not "settle" the Berlin
problem.

The Quadripartite Agreement on Berlin was signed in
September 1971. For the most part it formalized the
de facto situation that had existed since 1961. No
longer was there to be the concept of "Greater Berlin."
East Berlin was tacitly excluded from the main provisions of the document. West Berlin was guaranteed
improved travel to and from West Germany and enhanced
communications with all of Germany. The price paid by
West Germany and West Berlin for these concessions was
strict limitations on the legal ties between the two.
An annex to the Agreement specifically proscribes West
German political officials from performing official
duties in West Berlin.39/

The Agreement of course leaves West Berlin under
the sovereign control of the three Western powers of
World War II. This anachronism, some 26 years after the
close of the war and still more so today, reflected the
arduous difficulty involved in achieving any final
settlement in Berlin. Yet even the rather limited
Agreement of 1971 was an enormous improvement over
previous conditions and involved tortuous diplomacy.

The negotiations for the Quadripartite Agreement
were set in motion by President Nixon in West Berlin in
February 1969. He declared that the situation in Berlin
was "not satisfactory and ought to be regarded by every-
body as a call to action."40/ The United States,

---

38. Ibid., p. 256.

39. For further details and interpretations of the Quad-
ripartite Agreement, see Dennis L. Bark, Agreement on
Berlin (Washington, DC and Stanford, CA: American Enter-
prise Institute and the Hoover Institution, 1974);
Honore M. Catudal, Jr., A Balance Sheet of the Quadri-
partite Agreement on Berlin (Berlin [West]: Berlin
Verlag, 1978) and The Diplomacy of the Quadripartite
Agreement on Berlin (Berlin [West]: Berlin Verlag,
1978); and Ernst R. Zivier, The Legal Status of the Land
Berlin (Berlin [West]: Berlin Verlag, 1980).

40. Karl E. Birnbaum, East and West Germany: A Modus

realizing that extrication from Vietnam would be long and tortuous, sought to stabilize the situation in Europe and develop a working arrangement with the Soviet Union. The USSR was also interested in settling the most important outstanding issues in central Europe and in cultivating better relations with the United States. Hence, five months after Nixon's call for action Soviet Foreign Minister Gromyko signaled his government's readiness to negotiate. Both Britain and France saw a good opportunity to reduce tensions in Berlin, and the West German government, now pursuing Foreign Minister Brandt's Ostpolitik, welcomed the negotiations with enthusiasm. The Soviet Union was apparently very interested both in the negotiations and in Willy Brandt. At one point the Soviet ambassador to East Berlin even asked Brandt to try to build a small coalition so that the USSR would have as Chancellor someone to work with who was "a fresh man, no revanchist."41/

Walter Ulbricht saw all of this activity from a decidedly different perspective. The GDR under Ulbricht was the only actor involved in the Berlin negotiations that would have preferred no negotiations. It had little hope through this means of neutralizing West Berlin's destabilizing effect on the GDR, but it had much to lose. The Soviet Union had ten years earlier relented under tremendous pressure from Ulbricht. Now the situation was reversed. The Soviet Union and other Warsaw Pact allies had too much to gain from detente and a more forthcoming West Germany to permit Ulbricht to stand in the way. In 1969 Poland had followed Rumania in establishing diplomatic relations with the Federal Republic and, significantly, breaking with the standard GDR policy toward West Berlin.42/ The Soviets then began to threaten the GDR with a reduced role in alliance policymaking if it remained intransigent.43/ Eventually the conflict of interest between the GDR and the USSR grew to such dimensions that Ulbricht's ouster was ordered.44/ The Soviets thus cleared the way to negotiate the Berlin Agreement with a more loyal, less

-----

Vivendi (Lexington, MA: Lexington Books, 1973), p. 11.

41. Baring, Machtwechsel, p. 244.

42. Windsor, Germany and the Management of Detente, p. 186.

43. See Baring, Machtwechsel, p. 258.

44. See Heinz Lippmann, Honecker and the New Politics of Europe, trans. Helen Sebba (New York: Macmillan, 1972), pp. 217-224.

independent figure: Erich Honecker.

Honecker's accession to power in May 1971 removed the principal obstacle for the final, very difficult negotiations. Working from positions hardened by thirty years of conflict made compromise difficult, but eventually all parties worked out an agreement that fulfills the essential prerequisites formulated by Windsor almost a decade earlier.45/ The Quadripartite Agreement did not settle the Berlin problem. By any measure it simply improved conditions at the margin. Yet this alone made a great deal of difference to the beleaguered citizens of West Berlin. In the preface of a book celebrating "the relaxation of Berlin" Rolf Heyen related the meaning of the agreement from West Berlin's perspective:

> Berliners can telephone through the wall whenever they want.   They can visit friends without great difficulties. Freight shipments are no longer exposed to strict control. The Berlin traveler pays no toll now. The existence of the city is secured . . . From the threatened Berlin of the Khrushchev Ultimatum we have not seen the "free city" emerge. Rather Berliners can breathe more freely, and the ties between Berlin and the Federal Republic have been confirmed . . . The wall is still standing, but it has become more permeable. Berliners can, after a quarter of a century, go on to their own agenda."46/

The Reaction of the East

The Quadripartite Agreement principally served the East as a basis for detente and the long-sought Western recognition of Soviet-imposed borders. The GDR stood after 1972 as the main Eastern actor on the Berlin question. It was the permeability of the wall (albeit one-sided) that had worried Walter Ulbricht. In the years since 1961 there had been comparatively fewer West German automobiles and other tangible evidence of Western affluence. Now there would be a relative flood of visitors and the consequences for the GDR were difficult to assess. In anticipation of these problems, the theme of the SED party congress in June 1971, the first one led by Honecker, was ways to increase the material

---

45. See Baring, _Machtwechsel_, pp. 332-355; and Kissinger, _White House Years_, pp. 823-833.

46.   Rolf Heyen, ed. _Die Entkrampfung Berlins_ (Hamburg: Rowohlt, 1972), p. 2.

22

standard of living in the GDR.47/ This was a popular change, and the consumption rates for higher quality foodstuffs and appliances rose impressively. At the same time the GDR enjoyed a long-sought by-product of the Berlin Agreement. Between 1972 and 1974 it won the international diplomatic recognition that had eluded it for more than twenty years. Even the United States (and West Germany to a limited degree) extended recognition, and the GDR (as well as the FRG) became a full member of the United Nations.

Almost immediately, however, the euphoria that gripped East Germany's leadership in the wake of its great wave of international recognition was abruptly interrupted. The Soviet Union, for decades an absolutely reliable supplier of petroleum and basic grains, began to reduce its exports. Allies were instructed to look elsewhere for these essential raw materials. Yet as the GDR sought to establish markets outside its own economic alliance, the world economic recession and oil shortage of the mid-1970s made the task far more difficult than expected. The effect on the GDR has been a steadily increasing dependence on the West, and in particular on West Germany.

East German policy since 1971 has sought to limit the effects of this growing economic dependence on the Federal Republic and to distance itself as a fully separate state. Berlin is central to this orientation. The GDR holds steadfastly, despite Western objection, that East Berlin is a constituent part of the GDR and is the nation's capital. By contrast, West Berlin is still described as an "independent political entity" that exists "on the territory of the German Democratic Republic."

In June 1979 the GDR voted to amend its election law of 1967 to allow the direct election of East Berlin deputies to the Volkskammer (People's Chamber, the national legislature). Three years later the first East Berlin deputies entered the Volkskammer with full voting rights. The West protested this violation of Berlin's formal Four-power status, but is powerless to do anything that has any likelihood of altering the GDR's course unless it is prepared for a serious confronta- tion. Ironically, the Federal Republic has a great deal more direct leverage over the GDR now than do the Western powers in Berlin, but it is reluctant to press for major political concessions. Rather, the West Germans have concentrated their efforts on humanitarian questions, access to Berlin, and continued co-operation.

---

47. See Bundesministerium fuer innerdeutsche Bezieh- ungen, DDR Handbuch (Cologne: Verlag Wissenschaft und Politik, 1979), pp. 205-212.

The GDR is in a precarious position. Its economic dependence on West Germany jeopardizes not only its own political independence, but its potential relationship with Moscow as well. This has become more apparent recently as Honecker has tried to co-opt the growing peace movement in the GDR.48/ The GDR's obligation to West Berlin and West Germany to allow access to its territory also places it in an uncomfortable position. In a policy obviously designed both to generate additional income and limit the potentially disruptive waves of Western visitors, the GDR in 1980 increased four-fold the cost (i.e., mandatory exchange amount) of visitation. But perhaps the greatest problem West Berlin creates for the GDR is the long-standing threat of Western radio and television signals. The continued existence of West Berlin forces the GDR to surrender the information monopoly that is a fundamental characteristic of states in the Soviet bloc. It bears, in this sense, a considerable political burden that is unique in Eastern Europe.

The Reaction of the West

West Germany benefited greatly from the Quadripartite Agreement. Its reaction could hardly have stood in starker contrast to the GDR's. While the East Germans sought to minimize the damage and delimit the concessions of the treaty, the West Germans used the agreement as a diplomatic springboard. From the outset, Berlin had been the center and linchpin of Ostpolitik. Yet its centrality came more from its role as first and foremost obstacle, not as a final goal or even most fundamental objective.49/

West German leaders publicly stress the symbiotic relationship that Berlin has with Ostpolitik.50/ In reality, however, the Federal Republic has never had the authority to play a powerful role in determining Berlin's status. West Berlin thus has become both an economic burden and a diplomatic hurdle. As Helmut Schmidt told the German Bundestag in 1979, the Quadripartite Agreement was an essential prerequisite to the

---

48. See, e.g., Fritz Fack, "Freundliches aus der DDR," _Frankfurter Allgemeine Zeitung_, December 16, 1983, p. 1.

49. See Michael Kreile, "Ostpolitik Reconsidered," in _The Foreign Policy of West Germany_, p. 124.

50. See, e.g., Helmut Schmidt, _Perspectives on Politics_, ed. Wolfram Hanrieder (Boulder, CO: Westview Press, 1982), pp. 42, 54, 128, 147, 270.

general detente that occurred in Europe in the 1970s.51/

The shifting governmental position on Berlin is matched by a change in the West German public mood that must appear ominous to West Berliners. Public opinion data collected in the Federal Republic indicate that the Berlin problem ceased being a salient issue for West German citizens beginning about 1969. In 1977, a majority of West Germans could not correctly identify the construction of the Berlin wall when presented with the question: "Fifteen years ago, on August 13, something significant happened in German history. Do you know what it was?"52/

This is not to say that Berlin has in any way been abandoned by the West. The Federal Republic pours increasing amounts of money into West Berlin each year and regularly seeks to integrate the city in various sectors of West German public and private life. The Western powers, for their part, also play a less public but very active role. The United States, United Kingdom, and France often reassert their commitment to West Berlin's military defense and government. They maintain at least the formal view that Berlin (both East and West) remains a Four-power responsibility, despite the USSR's claim that the Four-power status was destroyed by the West in 1948.

Yet all this Western support comes at an official military or political level. While this ensures for West Berlin a good measure of safety from traditional adversaries, it is of limited value in combatting serious long-term problems of economic and population decline, changing demographic structures, and a changing attitude base in the population.53/

INTERNATIONAL PROSPECTS FOR BERLIN

The period since the Quadripartite Agreement has been productive for both East and West Berlin. The two have perceived the collective interest that they share

---

51. Ibid., p. 147.

52. Elisabeth Noelle-Neumann, Allensbacher Jahrbuch der Demoskopie, 1976-1977 (Vienna: Verlag Fritz Molden, 1977), pp. 59, 193.

53. See, e.g., Gerhard Mensch, "Economic Perspectives for Berlin," in The Future of Berlin, ed. M.J. Hillenbrand (Montclair, NJ: Allanheld, Osmun, 1980), pp. 153-228; or Werner D. von der Ohe, "Urbanological Perspectives on Berlin," in ibid., pp. 81-152.

in a number of areas and have cooperated. Most recently, for example, West Berlin agreed (with West German financing) to buy and operate the western portion of the S-Bahn, an elevated railway system in the whole of Berlin that the East had operated since 1945. Cooperation between East and West, however, is always subject to the GDR's first priority of creating distance and maintaining its independence.

At a higher level, Berlin remains a problem both for East and West Germany and for East and West generally. The situation there is an anachronism of the cold war. As such, it remains a kind of thermometer of world politics. The Soviet bloc knows that it is vulnerable to harassment. Such harassment has in fact occurred often since the signing of the Quadripartite Agreement. Berlin's geography puts its access from the West at risk, and this will likely always remain a problem, no matter what sort of international legal agreements are reached. Thus Berlin is today no less an exposed military target than it ever has been, defended mainly by conditions that make any attack in the foreseeable future most unlikely, since a military conflict could easily widen beyond Berlin.

In this sense Berlin is at once a critical point in the East-West deterrence network and one of the most vulnerable sites in the world for serious international crisis. That the Berlin crises of the past have not continued is testimony mainly to the effect of the Berlin wall of 1961, the Quadripartite Agreement of 1971, and the mutual economic and military interest of East and West. It seems likely at this juncture that Berlin's situation will remain fundamentally unaltered and that the East will continue to base its policy upon a patient expectation of attrition in West Berlin. It is Berlin's peculiar fate in the postwar world to remain subject to forces of all kinds and at any instant, to be the source of serious military confrontation between the Soviet Union and the United States. No event or agreement over the past forty years has removed this possibility.

The West

2

The United States and Berlin

William E. Griffith

THE DEVELOPMENT OF POSTWAR RELATIONS

The present relationship between the United States and West Berlin has become one in which legal complexities are exceeded only by its crucial political and military nature to Washington, Bonn, and West Berlin, and only less to London and Paris.

In the beginning this was quite unintended, certainly by Nazi Germany and almost as much by the United States. The relationship arose out of a naive, dangerous American combination of unwarranted optimism about post-World War II Soviet policy toward the United States and the German question, and a grave underestimation of the vulnerability of a Four-power-occupied West Berlin in the midst of a Soviet zone. Those who have read the late Professor Philip Mosely's analysis of the discussions in the wartime European Advisory Commission in London, will know that Mosely, a trained historian of Europe, vainly anticipated most of the problems that later occurred. Particularly vexing were his fruitless efforts, and those of James Riddleberger and Robert Murphy, to persuade the head of the American delegation, the idealistic and naive Ambassador John Winant, of Moscow's aims. It was, of course, not only Winant's naivete. Rather, Roosevelt gave low priority to postwar planning. What little there was reflected his belief that an arrangement with Stalin, in general and on the German question, would be arrived at which would <u>inter alia</u> make it safe for a Four-power occupied Berlin to be within the Soviet occupation zone.

In fact, this status of Berlin was predetermined by the agreement of the European Advisory Commission to a British-proposed zonal demarcation line, which put Mecklenberg, Saxony, and Thuringia in the Soviet zone. This was agreed to by the United States, notably by the U.S. military, because it feared, quite unjustifiably as it turned out, that the Soviet armies would end up even farther west than that, and that therefore such a demarcation line would help get the Red Army back from where it would likely reach its western limit. In fact, as it turned out, the British and American armies occupied much of the western part of the Soviet zone and were pulled back, shortly after the end of hostilities, and against Churchill's strong urgings, by the new President Truman. (Churchill wanted to force Stalin to make some concessions on Poland before the Allied armies were withdrawn, but Stalin was not asked for any, and of course made none.)

We now know that during the last stages of the war the emigre German communist leadership in Moscow, under Soviet direction, was planning maximally for the sovietization of the all of Germany and minimally of its Soviet zone. In my own judgment Stalin never wavered, except propagandistically, from these objectives, even in his 1952 offer, and because he soon realized that the first was impractical, he turned to the second one, which his successors, from Khrushchev to Gorbachev, have maintained. This, the sovietization of the Soviet zone, implied that sooner or later Four-power control of Germany would collapse and West Berlin would be isolated within the Soviet zone.

Western, and particularly American policy, accelerated this result. The Soviet-American cold war, let it be remembered, did not begin in, or about, West Berlin or Germany, but about the Soviet refusal to withdraw their troops from the northern Iranian province of Azerbayjan. Truman's firmness and the young Shah's Machiavellianism got them out in 1946, but much bad blood remained between Moscow and Washington. It was increased by the tensions between the two about the occupation of the divided Korean peninsula. The general change in the U.S. attitude about the Soviet Union from cooperation to hostility, and the rise of conservatism in the United States, combined with the sovietization of Moscow's zone, led Washington, under strong Congressional pressure, to decide that indefinite subsidization of the diet of West Germans by the U.S. taxpayer must be replaced by a recovery of the West German economy which would enable it to export enough to pay for its food imports. This led directly to the creation of the Bizonal and then Trizonal economic authorities, and in summer 1948 to the currency reform in the three Western zones, which the Soviets found a useful pretext for splitting the city of Berlin and initiating the first Berlin crisis.

An important, and this time primarily a German event had occurred in Berlin two years before, when the West German SPD (Sozialdemokratische Partei Deutschlands), led by Kurt Schumacher, frustrated the efforts of the Soviets, the German communists, and some East German SPD collaborators, led by Otto Grotewohl, to

merge the SPD and KPD (Kommunistische Partei Deutschlands) throughout Germany, or at least in the Soviet
zone and in all of Berlin, under KPD control. Ironically enough, both the American government and the CDU
(Christliche Demokratische Union) were little involved
in this. It was therefore Schumacher and the SPD which
first began the cold war in Germany, because it was the
only alternative which it had to being swallowed up.
(It should be added that a few left-wing anti-communists
in the American military government, including, if my
memory does not fail me, the then Captain Melvin Lasky,
did their part to help Schumacher and the West Berlin
SPD to resist Soviet pressure.) The vote in the West
Berlin SPD against the merger was overwhelming. This
was the first time, but far from the last, that the West
Berlin population itself made so clear its rejection of
the East German system and that the traditional American
adherence to self-determination, plus growing American
anti-communism, moved Washington to support West Berlin
more firmly than it otherwise might have.1/

There were significant differences of opinion among
the U.S. officials dealing with the Berlin blockade.
General Clay and Ambassador Murphy, then the senior U.S.
officials in Berlin, believed that military force should
be used to break it, because the Soviets were in no
position to retaliate, since the U.S. still had a
nuclear monopoly. The Joint Chiefs of Staff and
Secretary of the Army Royall thought that the city could
not be held militarily and that its evacuation should
seriously be considered. One of President Truman's
greatest and most fateful decisions was that the city
must be held by an airlift. It was, with the
enthusiastic support of its population, led by Mayor
Ernst Reuter. The Soviets abandoned the blockade in
1949. Ambassador Murphy wrote in his memoirs that he
thought that he should have resigned on this issue.2/ In
my own judgment he and General Clay were right: A
strong show of force would then have averted much worse
trouble later, including perhaps the Korean War.

The blockade ended with the city split and West
Germany in the process of becoming the Federal Republic.
This is not the place, nor am I the person, to discuss
the results of these events for the legal status of all
of Berlin and of the three Western sectors in

---

1. See chapter 10 in this volume for a more complete
account; or see Richard L. Merritt and Ronald A. Francisco, "The SPD of East Berlin, 1945-1961," Comparative Politics 5:1 (October 1972):1-28.

2. Robert D. Murphy, Diplomats Among Warriors (Garden
City: Doubleday, 1964), p. 317.

particular. Suffice it to say that Washington, Paris, and London, the occupying Powers in the western sectors of the city, and Bonn agreed to disagree on the matter. The Basic Law of the Federal Republic includes West Berlin as one of its constituent states. The three Western Allies suspended this part of the Basic Law, but in fact West Berlin largely is a part of the Federal Republic and could not survive without Bonn's massive economic subsidies. Nevertheless, sovereignty in the city remains in the hands of the occupying Powers, as the Quadripartite Agreement was to affirm in the 1970s. An increasingly effective consultation mechanism among the four Western Powers, the U.S., the U.K., France, and the Federal Republic, the so-called "Bonn group", gradually improved Allied-West German coordination. However, in time of crisis involving West Berlin, the importance of the United States vis-à-vis the Federal Republic is bound to, and always has increased. Washington gives much higher priority to the city; and the level of disagreements between Washington and Bonn about Berlin has usually risen, as well as that of disagreements within the Washington bureaucracy. Conversely, during periods of detente, things have gone much more smoothly and Berlin becomes an instrument of it rather than an obstacle to its continuation.

The former did not occur during the first Berlin crisis because that was almost entirely in the hands of the Americans and because the German official most directly concerned, Mayor Reuter, strongly supported American policy. But serious strains between Washington and Bonn developed during the second half of the second Berlin crisis, from 1958 to 1962. They deserve consideration in some detail because they foreshadowed the closer relations between Bonn and Paris, and the strains between Bonn and Washington, which characterized the late 1970s.

Khrushchev precipitated the second Berlin crisis in 1958 by declaring that Moscow would sign a peace treaty with East Germany and that West Berlin would thereafter have to depend for access on East Germany and would become a "free city," i.e., that its ties with the Federal Republic would be severed. The first part of the crisis was during the last years of the Eisenhower administration. While Chancellor Adenauer got along famously with Foster Dulles, he became distrustful of Eisenhower because of the Geneva summit meeting between him and Khrushchev and because he sensed, correctly, that Eisenhower, and even more the British and French, were lowering their priority for German reunification in favor of greater priority for arms control negotiations with the Soviets. Indeed, Adenauer's establishment of diplomatic relations between Bonn and Moscow was intended in part to reinsure the Federal Republic against this development.

Khrushchev wanted minimally to stabilize East Germany (which he did in 1961 with the Berlin wall) and maximally to destabilize West Germany. In 1962 he installed Soviet missiles in Cuba not only to try to catch up rapidly with the U.S. nuclear potential but also to try to force Washington to compromise, or even to capitulate, on the issues at stake in Berlin. As we know, he failed, and after he failed in Cuba the Berlin crisis rapidly evaporated.

But before that the new U.S. President Kennedy had made proposals to his allies, notably concerning the so-called International Access Authority, which could in my judgment have weakened the status of West Berlin and would only have whetted Khrushchev's appetite for more concessions. (True, Kennedy also raised the level of U.S. military mobilization, and I do not consider his inaction at the time of the construction of the Berlin wall to have been reprehensible, for the United States had neither a vital interest nor the military capability to change the situation in East Berlin or East Germany.) Kennedy's proposals excited the strong suspicions of Adenauer, who was in any case inclined to look unfavorably on the young, liberal President. General de Gaulle was equally suspicious and, moreover, realized that he thus had a unique opportunity to draw Adenauer away from Washington and toward him by taking an unrelentingly strong line on West Berlin. Thus Adenauer, via de Gaulle, as well as directly, effectively--and in my view fortunately--vetoed Kennedy's proposals. (I should add that Adenauer did not in fact want to run any major danger of war because of West Berlin, less than Kennedy did, but he agreed with de Gaulle that a rigid stand was the best way to force the Soviets to back down without war.)

From 1962 until 1969 the situation within and around West Berlin was relatively tranquil. The Vietnam War had displaced American attention toward southeast Asia. Despite it, detente with the Soviet Union continued, in part, as we can now see, because of the Sino-Soviet split and of Moscow's desire to prevent Washington from exploiting it to its, and Beijing's, advantage. Moreover, as we now know, 1962 was the beginning, behind the scenes, of the Cultural Revolution, and it was not until 1969, with the major Sino-Soviet border incidents of that year, that it tapered off. Thereafter, with Nixon and Kissinger in power in Washington, secret Sino-American negotiations began for a rapprochement on a common anti-Soviet platform and were sealed with success by Kissinger's surprise visit to Beijing in July 1971.

Before that, however, one little understood event involving West Berlin had showed that the city's fate was affected by global, and indeed east Asian politics. In the spring of 1969 the election of a new President of the Federal Republic was scheduled to occur, as usual, in West Berlin. Moscow and East Berlin raised strong objections to it and the Soviet Air Force began to make demonstrative flights over West Berlin. Then the first major Sino-Soviet border incident, on the Ussuri River, occurred. The Soviets immediately broke off their harassment of West Berlin, the Presidential election proceeded undisturbed, and a week later, unprecedentedly, the Soviet ambassador briefed the Federal Chancellor on the Soviet view of the Ussuri incident. It thus became clear that the Soviets had no intention of having crises on the western and eastern flanks simultaneously.

The state of Sino-Soviet relations was also one factor, albeit in my opinion a secondary one, in the conclusion of the Berlin Agreement in 1971. One major reason for it was the desire of the Soviets to get West German and then multilateral Western recognition of their sphere of influence in Eastern Europe, and especially East Germany. The other major reason was the desire of the new SPD-FDP government in Bonn, with Brandt as Chancellor and Scheel as foreign minister, to achieve detente with Moscow and East Berlin, with the double (and sometimes conflicting) aim of furthering detente in general and in central Europe in particular. Also, they stressed "maintaining the substance of the nation," i.e., establishing closer human and economic ties between West and East Germany so that the sense of a common German national consciousness would not erode further, but perhaps intensify. Bonn intended to recognize the status quo, but it was, as Egon Bahr said, in order to change it. The Soviets and East Germans, it goes without saying, shared the former aim, but not the latter, except insofar, as we can now see, that they expected to use the latter, including whatever success it might have, to put pressure on the Federal Republic later in order to prevent its policies from again becoming more unfavorable to Soviet and East German interests.

West Berlin thus became a crucial element in the complex negotiations involving the negotiation, signing, and ratification of the German treaties (with Moscow, Warsaw, East Berlin, and Prague, in that order) because Bonn and Washington both realized that the treaties would inevitably enable East Germany, if the Soviets did not stop it, to have more influence over the access routes to West Berlin. They therefore insisted that a new Four-power agreement on Berlin was a precondition for the treaties. (They also successfully made MBFR a precondition for agreeing to CSCE.) As the Berlin negotiations proceeded, it became clear that Moscow had much more interest than East Berlin in a new agreement. Basically, Bonn, Washington, and in the end, Moscow, were prepared for a compromise, whereby in return for a very partial limitation on the West German presence in

West Berlin, the Soviets would formally guarantee the security of access routes as a part of their Four-power responsibility for all of Germany and therefore for Berlin. Ulbricht, on the other hand, understandably felt that such an agreement would give away one of his major cards in putting pressure on Bonn. It was an indication of the Soviet interest in the German treaties and in detente with the United States in general that Moscow was prepared to remove Ulbricht in order to end the East German sabotage of the Berlin negotiations, which thereupon were successfully concluded. The Berlin question, that is, the status and security of, and access to West Berlin, have indeed since been defused.

Too much so? Has Berlin lost an empire and not yet found a role, as Acheson said about Great Britain? It is, I suppose, too early to tell. Nor am I aware of any convincing indications that this problem, if indeed it be one, is regarded by the United States as a major or even a serious one. One did, of course, note in West Berlin in the 1970s an intensified version of the "demobilization of detente" which helped to give rise to the protest wave, centering in Protestant, pietist Europe, which strongly opposed INF deployment. It would be difficult to imagine the Alternativen entering the West Berlin parliament during a Berlin crisis. Nor could one easily imagine so many Hausbesetzungen occurring then. And yet, I do not consider these developments an argument for returning to the cold war in Europe, something which I think would be not only be contrary to the fervent wishes of most West Europeans, and indeed, I should suspect, most West Berliners, but one in which my judgment is contrary to American interests as well.   Nor am I advocating that the United States, with or without the British and French, should undertake itself some new initiative about West Berlin. In view of the geographic isolation and consequent military vulnerability of the U.S. garrison in West Berlin, and of the military impossibility of West Germany defending the city, it seems to me that the Berlin Agreement and, in general, its implementation to date have been about the best that West Berlin, Bonn, and Washington could have hoped to get. Moreover, the Berlin Agreement, in which Washington and Moscow played the most important roles, is a major component of detente in Europe. If the latter erodes, the former is likely to erode also. Thus the very vulnerability of West Berlin, and of the American military forces stationed there, makes detente in central Europe all the more important to Washington and Bonn. As we now can see more clearly than at the time of the German treaties, where their interests diverge with respect to the GDR, to which Bonn is bound to give a higher priority than is Washington. Bonn has a major, if seldom expressed long-range interest, as Egon Bahr put it, to change and in the short-run to have closer relations with the GDR. Washington, however, has less interest in East Germany. Indeed, Washington's interest in changing the status quo in the GDR arises primarily because this is a policy of one of its major allies, the Federal Republic.

CONTEMPORARY POLICY CONSIDERATIONS

West Germany and the United States, and therefore of necessity West Berlin as well, are now confronted with a largely new set of circumstances. The U.S., West Germans, and West Berliners are vulnerable as a result of their and their allies' energy dependence on oil coming largely from the Persian Gulf area. In large part because of the great rise in the price of this oil in 1973 and 1979, but also because of unwise economic policies by the United States, all three were confronted by a crisis of stagflation in the early 1980s. Political stability in the Federal Republic, and perhaps even more in West Berlin, has until very recently had the silent support of the West German <u>Wirtschaftswunder</u>. This now seems over. Simultaneously, the United States is calling for a rapid rise in West German defense expenditures, as it is engaged in itself, even if, as some Administration members--unwisely--added this means cuts in West German social services. Even if Reagan, Schmidt, and now Kohl, seem determined to improve the style of West German-American relations, which so deteriorated during the Carter administration, the differences of substance, notably on defense expenditures, East-West trade, and most other aspects of Western policies toward the Soviet Union, remain important.

Within this context, ironically enough, West Berlin remains one of the ties that bind Washington and Bonn. No elected West German government could possibly afford to abandon West Berlin. Yet Bonn cannot possibly defend it; only the United States can. I would myself argue that from the point of view of its own national interests the United States cannot afford to abandon West Berlin. American public support for continued American presence in West Berlin remains high.

But to say this is not to face up to the central problem. As we have seen, in moments of East-West crisis, the Berlin crisis can assume a more serious dimension. The present crisis is new in one respect which affects West Berlin and the United States. For the first time Bonn now takes a considerably less alarmed view of Soviet policy than Washington does, and Washington's priority is no longer in Europe, but in the Middle East or arguably in the Pacific Basin. (One may argue that Kissinger was initially suspicious of

Brandt's <u>Ostpolitik</u>--and has recently become so again-- but this was a brief period and <u>Ostpolitik</u> was finally carried out with much American support and assistance.) Were the Soviet Union to try to put pressure on Berlin in such a situation, would Washington respond as rapidly and decisively as Bonn might like it to? Or more so than Bonn would like? Or, for that matter, could one not argue that Bonn's policy of maintaining Europe as a island of detente is one reason exactly why Moscow does not put pressure on Berlin at present?

It is too early to answer these questions, and in my judgment any one may turn out to have been correct. The main reason that we cannot answer them is that crises remain in Eastern Europe essentially unresolved. Indeed, as the Soviet Union increasingly faces chal- lenges in much of Eastern Europe, we have seen the surprising East-West German entente and Soviet uncertainty. It is thus Soviet hegemony over Eastern Europe, Soviet-American relations, and Soviet-West German relations, also a renewed Berlin crisis that are now at stake in the events still unfolding in Eastern Europe.

3

Western Europe and West Berlin

Roger Morgan and Caroline Bray

GENERAL PERSPECTIVES

The perspectives of West European governments on the problem of Berlin are shaped by their views on the larger problems of Europe, including the German question and the issues of East-West relations. For the European capitals most directly concerned with Berlin, namely Paris and London, attitudes to Berlin derive partly from the position of France and the United Kingdom in the Western alliance (together with the United States and the Federal Republic of Germany [FRG]), partly from their legal position as victors in the Second World War (together with the United States and the USSR), and partly from their membership of the European Community (together with the FRG).

This combination of relationships, especially the status of World War II victors, gives France and Britain a direct responsibility for Berlin, and this chapter focuses especially on French and British views. Their general perspective on the Berlin problem, however, is shared by other countries in Western Europe, particularly other members of NATO. These other countries share the French and British attitude of general support for the FRG's <u>Ostpolitik</u>, in the wider context of the Western alliance's relations with the Soviet bloc, and their attitude toward the present and future role of Berlin is shaped by their attitude toward these wider questions.

The French and British positions with regard to Berlin are based firmly on their legal status as two of the Powers exercising quadripartite control over the whole of Berlin by virtue of the agreements of September 12 and November 14, 1944. Even though this quadripartite control over Berlin has, of course, ceased to exist <u>de facto</u>, the French and British view (like that of the United States) is that it remains valid <u>de jure</u>, and this view was not affected by the practical arrangements agreed upon in the Quadripartite Agreement of September 1971.

The connection between the legal rights of the Western Allies and their political relationship to their West German allies (including West Berliners) was summarized by President Giscard d'Estaing during his visit to West Berlin in October 1979, when he used the formula "the rights of the Allies represent the liberty of the Berliners." This unusually explicit expression of France's legal rights in Berlin did not denote any difference in substance between the views of all three of the Western Allies, namely, that Berlin's special status must be preserved.

There appear to be several reasons for the strong insistence by Britain and France on their interpretation of the legal status of all of Berlin. First, France and Britain, like the United States, maintain their legal rights and military and other responsibilities in Berlin because of their relationship with the Federal Republic, and the wish and need of Germans and Berliners that they should be there: to depart from this position would, in effect, allow two million Berliners to be absorbed into the GDR. Second, any renunciation of British or French rights and responsibilities might strengthen the Soviet view that quadripartite responsibility as a whole should be ended. Third, any such renunciation would reduce British and French influence in seeking a long-term solution to the German question (perhaps reunification), and would perhaps also reduce their influence in the short run over the evolution of relations between their ally the FRG and the GDR. Fourth, the co-responsibility of Britain and France for the status and security of Berlin helps to consolidate their ties with the United States and the FRG, and the regular consultations of the four foreign ministers on Berlin problems may provide a convenient forum for the discussion of other alliance issues as well. (The semi-annual meetings at the Foreign Minister level should not be confused with the more technical meetings of the so-called "Bonn Group," in which the four countries are represented at the official level.)

These factors, to which others would be added, explain the insistence of Britain and France on their rights and responsibilities in Berlin. This view has led to several consequences, including the insistence of the occupying Powers since 1949 that "Land Berlin" is not part of the FRG, and their maintenance of special procedures for the application in West Berlin of federal legislation and regulations. Although the West European allies of the FRG support the view that West Berlin should be integrated as closely as possible into the economy, society, and political system of the FRG (including, for instance, accepting West Berlin's representation in the Bundestag and the Bundesrat, and the FRG's representation of Berlin abroad), they insist that federal legislation can be applied in Berlin only if the Allies do not object.

The Western legal position was maintained throughout the negotiation of the Quadripartite Agreement in 1970-71, and the three Western signatories of that agreement have always insisted that it did not change the fundamental legal status of Berlin. The Soviet Union, however, claims that the treaty established a new basis for West Berlin's status as an independent entity, entirely separate from the FRG.

The Quadripartite Agreement has brought fifteen years of relative stability to Berlin's international situation, and this has been particularly striking during the period of renewed East-West tension during the late 1970s and early 1980s. For the countries of Western Europe, faced with the disappointments of the CSCE, MBFR, and SALT processes, and the threats represented by rising East-West tension in general and the Polish situation in particular, the fact that Berlin is not now a source of East-West conflict, as it so often was between 1948 and 1970, is a great relief.

The Western European countries attach great importance to the maintenance of this calm situation around Berlin, and their policies must be influenced by their assessment of why the USSR and the German Democratic Republic (GDR) have continued a moderate line towards Berlin, despite the rise in East-West tension elsewhere.

As seen from Western Europe, it appears that the recent Soviet (and GDR) moderation towards Berlin may be motivated by five considerations (some of which, indeed, may already have induced Khrushchev to terminate an earlier Berlin crisis in 1963): First, time may be on the Eastern side, in the sense that the (very long-term) economic and demographic weakening of West Berlin might ultimately allow the city to fall under Soviet influence without any need to provoke a crisis. Second, both the USSR and the GDR draw advantages (including West German credits) from current East-West economic dealings, which might be compromised by a Berlin crisis. Third, the status quo gives the Soviet Union a valuable _droit de regard_ in relation to the whole future development of Germany, and this would be less easy to exercise when tension escalated in and around Berlin. Fourth, West Berlin may appear as a hostage, a security, which can be exploited by the USSR or the GDR to obtain co-operative behavior (especially by the FRG, but perhaps by other Western states too), on issues such as theater nuclear modernization or possible Western intervention in support of Poland, and this effect will only prevail as long as the threat to disrupt Berlin's relations with the West is invoked but not implemented; and finally, it may appear to the USSR and the GDR that any renewed Berlin crisis would cement the solidarity of the West in general.

As the basis of this kind of assessment of Soviet interests and perceptions, the Western European countries have a clear interest in maintaining firmness on their basic positions while carefully refraining from any action which might provoke the Eastern side into departing from its present moderate attitude. (Maintaining peaceful relations with West Germany and the Western Allies does not prevent the Soviet Union from pressing its own contrary legal interpretations, which, if conceded to in any way, might make the Allied position untenable.)

For these and other reasons, Britain and France are inclined to combine the strongest possible political support for West Berlin with clear reaffirmations of their legal rights and responsibilities, in order to ensure that the USSR has no possible pretext for challenging the Western legal position or unleashing a new crisis.

This double concern--to support West Berlin's political and economic viability while safeguarding against any possible infringement of their own legal position-- is clearly illustrated by the attitude of France and Britain towards the evolution of West Berlin's role in the European Community.

THE EUROPEAN COMMUNITY

<u>Economic Integration</u>

The fact that West Berlin is included in the FRG's membership in the European Community gives the West Berliners political, psychological, and economic advantages. If West Berlin had not been included, the city would have faced barriers to its trade with the European Community as a whole and even with its natural and primary economic partner, the Federal Republic.

Direct financial support from the EC to Berlin is very modest in comparison with the substantial subsidies which the city receives from the FRG. Nevertheless, some large grants have been received: from 1977 to 1985 DM 139.1 million from the European Social Fund largely for training of the unemployed and young people; a range of grants for research and bursaries in technical institutes; and a total of DM 110 million in loans from the European Investment Bank for Electricity and Gas Supply installations.

The European Regional Development Fund produced DM 15.1 million between 1976 and 1979 to help build a refuse disposal plant at Neukoelln, and in 1980 DM 39.75 million towards the modernized Exhibition and Trade Fair Halls. In 1985 a grant of DM 53.3 million was made to the Berlin Center for Innovation and New Enterprises for industrial investment. The member states of the Community participate in the great range of trade events and congresses held in Berlin, and the Community as such participates and gives financial support to such major events as the International Tourist Exchange, the International Green Week, and the Overseas Import Fair (which helps developing countries show their goods in Europe).1/

The Community and its members are happy to make use of Berlin's unique geographical position for such events. Many have good attendance from state-trading nations, all of which have trade offices in East Berlin, and many in West Berlin. Many West European countries have a steady two-way trade with Berlin, and in 1982 about 41 percent of Berlin's exports went to EC member states.

It would seem therefore, that West Berlin has an assured place in West European trade and as a center for East-West trade contacts, and can count on a steady, if modest, flow of funds from Brussels to support social and infrastructure projects in the city.

The Legal and Historic Basis

In accordance with the procedure whereby the Federal Republic includes Berlin in its international treaties, the FRG attached to the Treaty of Rome (1957) a declaration on ratification, to the effect that the treaties establishing the European Economic Community and the European Atomic Energy Community would apply equally to West Berlin, and that "this declaration does not affect the rights and responsibilities of France, the United Kingdom and the United States regarding Berlin." The Allied military government acknowledged Berlin's inclusion in a letter to the Senate of November 18, 1957, raising no objection in so far as this was compatible with their rights and responsibilities, which must be regarded as paramount, and stating that Allied legislation was not affected.2/

Berlin's inclusion in the European Community hinges on the declarations by the FRG and the Allies; it must

---

1. Details of Community aid to West Berlin were supplied by the European Commission's Press and Information Office in Berlin.

2. For a full survey of Berlin's legal position in the European Community, see Ruediger Huette, "Berlin and the European Communities," Yearbook of European Law, vol. 3 (Oxford: Clarendon Press, 1984), pp. 1-23.

however be seen in relation to the continuance of Allied rights and responsibilities when considering the extent of power which the Community has directly over Berlin.

The FRG's partners in the Treaty of Rome defined their attitude in a joint declaration on Berlin, its special position and need of support. They confirmed their solidarity with the people of Berlin, and their intention to "use their good offices with the Community in order that all necessary measures may be taken to ease the economic and social situation of Berlin, to promote its development and to ensure its economic stability." It is on this basis that the Community institutions and the original six member states--later the Nine, the Ten, and now the Twelve--have been willing to grant requests for aid which come to the Commission from the Berlin Senate through official federal German channels, to the extent of making, wherever possible, a special case of Berlin. Perhaps the clearest example of this good will of the Communities is seen in the fact that in 1975, when the new European Regional Development Fund was introduced, Berlin was recognized as one of the areas for special assistance which could both receive Community aid, and for which there would be no limit set on the substantial states aid from the FRG.

Problems of European Community Legislation

There have, however, been problems for the Community and for the Western Allies from the extension of FRG's Community membership to Berlin (France and Britain being both EC partners and occupation Powers). One range of problems concerns the legislation passed by the Communities and adopted in Berlin, including trade and other treaties with countries outside the Community.

The nature of European Community law is complex. Particularly the process whereby it, like federal German law, is adopted, with Allied Kommandatura approval, by the Berlin parliament and government, is the subject of some debate among lawyers. We cannot explore it fully here. In practical terms, though, where EC acts are the subject of federal German legislation, long-standing procedures exist to ensure that Allied rights and responsibilities are safeguarded.

Also important are European Community regulations and certain other instruments which come into force directly. These are enacted throughout the Community, and there are specific procedures laid down to ensure that the Allies are informed of the regulation in time to take action if it would affect an area of their responsibility. In fact the subject matter of Community legislation has thus far hardly concerned such areas as security and defense, and the status of West Berlin and its citizens continues to be safeguarded by Allied reserved powers.

One area in which the Allies reserve responsibility is that of Berlin's airspace. In the case of two recent EC Council directives concerning aviation, a procedure was adopted whereby the FRG informed the EC Council that, because of Allied reserved powers the directive did not cover Berlin, and the Allies for their part stated formally that the directive could not apply in relation to Berlin. This procedure was adopted following full consultation among all the states concerned. It reflects clearly the fact that occupation law ultimately prevails over European Community law in Berlin.3/

In the case of external treaties of the Community, complex questions arise. The main concern of the Allies here also has again been to ensure that they are adequately informed through Bonn government channels of impending treaties with third parties. Both from their and the Community's point of view, the Federal Republic's insistence that all new treaties should apply equally to Berlin, no matter how irrelevant the subject matter (Atlantic Fisheries agreements, for example) has caused some irritation.

A territorial application clause appended to all Community external treaties covers in general terms not only Berlin, but also such "outlying" areas as Gibraltar and British bases in Cyprus.4/ The Soviet view is that Community and other international treaties may only extend to West Berlin if they contain a specific Berlin clause which makes reference to the Quadripartite Agreement of 1971. This procedure was laid down by the so-called Frank-Falin formula devised by Bonn and Moscow in 1972, and its essential purpose from the Soviet point of view is to underline that West Berlin is not part of the FRG, or governed by it. The necessity for a reference to the Quadripartite Agreement is not accepted by the European Community, with the result that occasional problems have arisen during negotiation of EC treaties with countries supporting the Soviet viewpoint.

Berlin's Integration in the EC Institutional Framework

For the Berliners, dependent economically on the West and anxious to preserve their political ties with the Federal Republic, it is very important to demonstrate openly their membership in the Western world, including the European Community. The Community has responded in the spirit of its Treaty of Rome declara-

---

3. Ibid., pp. 1 and 18.

4. Ibid., p. 19.

tion with frequent demonstrations of its presence in West Berlin. In 1968, a Press and Information Office of the Commission was established. The Community decided in 1975, at the request of the Federal Republic, to locate the European Center for Vocational Training in Berlin. It was opened in 1977, and plays a role in research and coordination on a Europe-wide scale of schemes for career training and retraining.5/

Commission officials visit West Berlin frequently. Every Commission president visits Berlin at least once during his term and the Governing Mayor, in turn, visits Brussels. The Praesidium, party groups and committees of the European Parliament regularly hold meetings in Berlin, generally in the Reichstagsgebaeude. These events as well as the regular participation and co-financing by the Community in major exhibitions such as the International Green Week, attended by the Commissioner for Agriculture, underscore Berlin's involvement in the normal, day-to-day life of the European Community.

From the middle to late 1970s, however, the Soviet Union and the German Democratic Republic frequently objected that these demonstrations of European Community ties with Berlin are unacceptable, either because they were said to affect the existing situation of Berlin's status referred to in the Quadripartite Agreement, or on grounds that Berlin was not part of the Community. Their most outspoken and prolonged attacks were, however, reserved for the impending inclusion of Berlin members in the first directly elected European Parliament of 1979.6/

Berlin Members of the European Parliament

It was the vision of the original founders of the European Community eventually to create a supranational body with the fully democratic legitimacy conferred by an elected assembly. This vision seemed to move a step nearer reality with the decision in 1974 to introduce direct election of Members of the European Parliament. Berlin was allocated three representatives among the

---

5. See Berlin Report 5/83: Berlin in the European Community--The European Community in Berlin (Berlin [West]: Press and Information Office of the Land Berlin, 1983).

6. For a range of Soviet arguments, see P. Abrassimow, Westberlin gestern und heute (Berlin [East]: Staatsverlag der DDR, 1981); and Das vierseitige Abkommen ueber Westberlin und seine Realisierung, Dokumente 1971-1977 (Berlin [East]: Staatsverlag der DDR, 1977).

Federal Republic's group of 81. Although they were to be delegated by West Berlin's popular assembly (Abgeordnetenhaus), not directly elected, this was a considerable gain from the previous situation whereby Berlin was (usually but not always) allotted European Assembly representatives from among the members it sent to the Bundestag in Bonn.

The protests led by the Soviet Union against this development were founded on what seemed the very real possibility of an alteration in Berlin's status by involvement in a new democratic body which would play a central role in eventual European political union. This, it felt, could be tantamount to incorporation of West Berlin in the FRG "by the back door." The GDR countered what it saw as a change in West Berlin's status by arranging in 1979 for East Berlin members of its popular assembly (Volkskammer) to be directly elected in 1981.

The Western Allies have continued to maintain that, since the West Berlin members of parliament are _not_ directly elected, their participation in the European assembly does _not_ affect the status of Berlin. In practical terms, European political union is a long way off and the role of the Parliament is limited: It is still a consultative, and not a legislative body, and real power in the European Community still resides with the Council of Ministers of the member states. But the question remains, not only of increased powers for the European Parliament in the future, but of the extension of the Community's policy competence into fields such as defense spending, which might indeed affect Allied responsibilities and the status of Berlin. This issue is of concern as much to the Western Allies as to the Soviet Union.

CONCLUSION

It follows from this analysis that France, Britain, and other West European allies of the Federal Republic would like to see the economic viability and legal and political position of West Berlin maintained on the basis of Quadripartite Agreement and Allied legal rights, until such time as a peace settlement for the whole of Germany can be achieved.

There may indeed one day be some fundamental change in the structure of East-West relations in Europe which makes German reunification or some other solution for Germany (confederation?) acceptable to all the parties concerned, and which would thereby give a new status to Berlin. Unless and until such a change occurs, the states of Western Europe will continue their present policy.

4

Paris, Moscow
and the Berlin Problem

Renata Fritsch-Bournazel

France's foreign policy, at least since 1870, has been determined by the massive presence of Germany on her eastern border. Notwithstanding the greatly changed international system that resulted from the Second World War, the place occupied by Germany in Europe continued to be France's most important external problem, though the economic and political effects of the war prevented the French from playing any significant international role in trying to solve it. A medium-sized power such as France can exert relatively little influence within power blocs dominated by colossi like the United States or the Soviet Union, and French governments have generally worked for a more independent Europe in a multipolar global system.

The close involvement of the two superpowers in European affairs has modified the Franco-German relationship as much as the defeat of Hitler, but the maintenance of Allied rights and responsibilities has perpetuated France's special status as one of the four occupying powers in Germany. Quadripartism has been, throughout the period since the Second World War, one of the instruments of French foreign policy, in terms of the preservation and extension of the country's influence abroad.

French governments, seeking to safeguard their policy objectives, have sometimes attempted to use the Soviet Union as a balancing factor, as a possible counterweight to Germany or the United States. However, France's firm stand on the status of Berlin has not fundamentally altered since 1945, and her response to Soviet pressure on Berlin was capable of being more uncompromising than that of the British and Americans. For example, when the Soviet Union in November 1958 demanded that West Berlin be "free" and demilitarized, and followed this up with an ultimatum that the question must be settled by a conference within six months, French reaction, at least outwardly, was much more resolute than that of the other Western Allies of the

Federal Republic. During the Berlin crisis of 1961, acting on the assumption that it would be unwise to negotiate either over Berlin or about Germany while the Soviet Union was still issuing threats and peremptory orders to the West, de Gaulle counselled the postponement of talks until all Russian threats had ceased.1/

Twenty years later, in accord with de Gaulle's recipe for dealing with the Kremlin in periods of crisis, the attitude of the Mitterrand administration showed striking similarities with the firmness of Gaullist declarations at the time of the Berlin wall in 1961 and of the Cuban crisis in 1962. In the context of increased East-West tensions after Afghanistan and the Soviet military buildup in Europe, France clearly stood for a hard line against Soviet attempts to bully the Western Alliance. According to Foreign Minister Cheysson, the perspectives of the French government on East-West issues, including the Berlin problem, are dictated by the fact that the Socialists "are firmly against any form of totalitarianism, any threat to other people and countries."2/

FRANCE'S STATUS AS AN OCCUPYING POWER

The main reason for France's insistence on her rights and responsibilities in Berlin is her wish to preserve a valuable _droit de regard_ in relation to any future development of the German question. Quadripartite control over Berlin, even though it has ceased to exist de facto,3/ is the most tangible manifestation of France's legal position as a victor in the Second World War, a position for which General de Gaulle had been struggling so hard. To a considerable extent, indeed, French policy towards Germany in the immediate postwar period has been a response to agreements concluded without the participation of French representatives, and frequently without the consideration of French interests. At Teheran, neither Stalin nor Roosevelt was keen to elevate the French to a position

---

1. Press Conference, 5 September 1961, in Charles de Gaulle, _Discours et messages_ (Paris: Plon, 1970), pp. 335-337.

2. Interview with H.E. Bilges and J. Leibel, _Bild_, July 10, 1981.

3. For the basic legal views of the four Allies see Pierre Maurel, Les compétences des Alliés à Berlin (Toulouse, 1980). Ph.D. dissertation.

of international importance by giving them an occupation zone in Germany. General de Gaulle, a week before his government received official recognition from the Allies, demanded representation for his country in the three-power European Advisory Commission (EAC), which had been given the dual task of preparing the terms of the German surrender and of suggesting the machinery for their implementation. But the demand for a French occupation zone was still at that stage turned down by both Roosevelt and Stalin. It was not until after de Gaulle's Moscow visit at the end of 1944 that the American president agreed in principle to granting the French such a zone.4/

In Moscow, de Gaulle had been seeking a special relationship with the Soviet Union, both to bolster his status in the eyes of the British and Americans, and to tame the French Communists.5/ The twenty-year Franco-Soviet treaty of December 1944, directed only against Germany, did not affect, however, Stalin's basic attitude about de Gaulle's international pretensions, particularly in his views on postwar Germany. At Yalta, in February 1945, Churchill pleaded vigorously for giving France a share in the occupation of Germany, to help shoulder Britain's overwhelming responsibility for the onerous task once the United States had withdrawn its forces from the continent. When the Soviet leader finally agreed,6/ it was only on the understanding that the French occupation zone would come out of the Anglo-American area. Similarly, the Russians succeeded in having the French sector in the German capital carved out of the previously agreed British and American portions. French protests in Moscow about their being

---

4. Cf. Herbert Tint, _French Foreign Policy since the Second World War_ (London: Weidenfeld and Nicolson, 1972), pp. 34-39.

5. For the relevance of the triangular relationship among the French government, the French Communist Party and the Soviet Union, see Alfred Grosser, _Franco-Soviet Relations Today_ (Santa Monica: Rand Corporation, 1967), p. 12.

6. Interestingly enough, any reference to Stalin's ridicule of DeGaulle's great-power pretensions, as recorded in the American conference papers, was eliminated from the Soviet minutes published shortly after DeGaulle's state visit to the Soviet Union. Cf. _Tegeran-Yalta-Potsdam. Sbornik dokumentov_ (Moscow: Meždnunarodnye Otnošenja, 1967).

excluded from the Potsdam conference in July 1945,7/ which was to decide on problems like the delimitation of occupation zones in Germany, reparation procedures and population transfers, were also unavailing.

Rebuffed in their bid for influence, the French reluctantly endorsed the Potsdam decisions while pursuing an independent course. In a note of August 1945, the French government stated its refusal to allow a central administration to be set up in Germany and vetoed any expansion of the "central agencies" the Russians had erected in East Berlin.8/ The weakest of the occupying powers, France, managed to cut off her zone from the rest of Germany and envisaged partition as a desirable solution. By 1947, the French had to acknowledge the fiasco of their attempts at an independent foreign policy related to Germany. This policy had failed not only because of the increasing rift between the Soviet Union and the Anglo-American Allies9/ which reduced the problem of France's rank in the world to the determination of her position within the Western Alliance. At the meeting of Allied foreign ministers in Moscow, in 1947, Soviet opposition to most of the French demands in relation to Germany had made clear to France that even her basic economic needs could be satisfied only if she gave full support to the United States and Britain. Her urgent need for Saar and Ruhr coal and for economic aid had made independence a luxury she could not afford.10/

THE IMPACT OF THE BERLIN CRISES

In March 1948, the Russian representative broke up the Four-power Control Commission meeting in Berlin,

---

7. For a fuller exposition of the German question at Potsdam, see Renata Fritsch-Bournazel, L'Union Soviét-ique et les Allemagnes (Paris: Fondation nationale des sciences politiques, 1979), pp. 27-32.

8. Cf. Ernst Deuerlein, "Frankreichs Obstruktion deutscher Zentralverwaltungen 1945," Deutschland-Archiv 4 (1971): 466-491.

9. On the evolution of French opinion, see Klaus Haensch, Frankreich zwischen Ost und West. Die Reaktion auf den Ausbruch des Ost-West-Konflikts, 1946-1948 (Ber-lin, New York: de Gruyter, 1972. Ph.D. dissertation.

10. Cf. Alfred Grosser, Les Occidentaux. Les pays d'Europe et les Etats-Unis depuis la guerre (Paris: Fa-yard, 1978), p. 85.

thus ending the last joint East-West effort to implement the Potsdam arrangements for the postwar government of Germany. The blockade of Berlin imposed by the Russians at the end of June 1948 acted as a spur to further French collaboration with Britain and the United States. Since 1947, France's policy towards the Soviet Union had been increasingly aligned with that of her Western partners who tended at that time to present a monolithic front in their dealings with the Kremlin. In the light of the new international created by the Communist take-over in Czechoslovakia in February 1948 and the blockade of the former German capital four months later, the French government finally felt constrained to adopt the Anglo-American propositions for interzonal cooperation and the establishment of a West German government. Within a few days Berlin became the incarnation of freedom: Germany ceased to be a defeated country and became a partner. Moreover, the practical solidarity of the three Western Allies during the Berlin Airlift11/ in the face of what was perceived as a major Communist threat prepared the ground for the drive towards European integration.

Ten years later, the second Berlin crisis opened in a very different international setting. When Khrushchev launched his demands on Berlin in November 1958, just after de Gaulle's return to power, France tried to assume the role of Bonn's protector in the confrontation with the East. Against presumed American neglect of West European interests and Anglo-American readiness to allow the Russians to change the legal status of West Berlin, Adenauer resolved to strengthen Germany's ties with France. According to a tacit agreement between Adenauer and de Gaulle, the Federal Republic would help the French president in the assertion of European claims vis-à-vis the United States within NATO, while de Gaulle would support Adenauer's case with the Soviet Union whether on Berlin or on reunification.12/

Nevertheless, unlike de Gaulle, the German chancellor firmly believed that only a strong and manifestly united NATO could be a satisfactory deterrent to the Soviet Union, since the protection of West Berlin and the Federal Republic could only be assured with the

---

11. For a detailed account of French activities during the Berlin blockade, see the testimony of General Gane-val in Carrefour, May 6, 1959; and Charles Corcelle, Les Alliés occidentaux à Berlin depuis 1945 (Paris: Al-batros, 1976), pp. 168-182.

12. Alfred Grosser, La politique extérieure de la Ve République (Paris: Editions du Seuil, 1965), p. 85.

help of the United States.13/ The building of the Berlin Wall, on August 13, 1961, however, imparted a new degree of tension into the Germany-American relationship and helped de Gaulle to reinforce the Franco-German entente. Whereas the Americans and still more the British took the view that negotiation with the East was a logical and necessary was to reduce the potentially explosive situation in Berlin,14/ de Gaulle agreed to support Adenauer's attempts to resist Soviet pressures on Berlin and to refuse changes in Berlin's status or in access arrangements concerning the city that might have had the effect of conferring legitimacy on the East German regime. Whether in fact Adenauer and de Gaulle were willing to go further than the Americans and British in resisting the Soviet moves in Berlin remains an open question.

On several occasions, de Gaulle had made clear that he saw the Soviet difficulties with the consolidation of Eastern Europe, internal pressures for liberalization of the regime and the Sino-Soviet split as factors pushing the Russians to seek an agreement with the West.15/ But contrary to the reaction of France's allies, his recipe for dealing with the Kremlin appeared to be less indulgent than that of the United States and Britain. After having openly criticized direct Anglo-American contacts with the Soviet Union, he credited himself with having saved the West from a debacle. By refusing to negotiate on Berlin or Germany as long as the Soviet Union did not stop threats and injunctions, he stated, "We have avoided the worst for both our Allies and ourselves, whether that would have been in the form of a catastrophic climb-down, a dramatic break-down or a tragic-comic bogging-down."16/

---

13. See Edward A. Kolodziej, _French International Policy under de Gaulle and Pompidou: The Politics of Grandeur_ (Ithaca and London: Cornell University Press, 1974), pp. 235-272.

14. For the negative effect of the Berlin crisis on German-American relations, see Roger Morgan, _The United States and West Germany, 1945-1973: A Study in Alliance Politics_ (London: Oxford University Press, 1974), pp. 110-115.

15. See his press conferences of November 10, 1959 and September 5, 1961.

16. Charles de Gaulle, _Discours et messages_, vol. 3, p. 385.

THE OSTPOLITIK AND THE FOUR-POWER BERLIN TALKS

The construction of the Berlin Wall put an end to the realistic hope for the reunification of Germany and destroyed any perspective that the city of Berlin would soon again become the center of a united Germany. In fact, it had not really changed anything since the two parts of Germany had been separated before, and the West had no longer any real authority in East Berlin. The point was that the Wall ended illusions in the Federal Republic and forced the people and their leaders to concentrate on improving the status quo.17/ In March and April 1958, Adenauer had even tried to sound out Soviet interest in an "Austrian solution" for the GDR, thus focusing on the living conditions of the East Germans rather than institutional unity, but the Soviet leaders did not respond and Khrushchev's Berlin ultimatum of the same year closed the matter.18/ The most important contributions to the debate that shaped West German thinking were made however after the erection of the Berlin wall,19/ until they became official policy in 1966-1967.

Through his specific strategic proposals for dealing with the German problem in the European context, de Gaulle gave further momentum to the West German debate on priorities and carried it into the realm of alternative strategies. In 1959, he was the first Western statesman to recognize the Oder-Neisse line as the final frontier of a reunited Germany and, in 1965, the first to express clearly that a recognition of the frontiers--together with Germany's participation in European integration--was a precondition for progress towards Germany unity. De Gaulle believed that European and German unification could succeed only if the Soviet Union and Germany composed their differences, not as in 1922 against the Western countries, but in accord with them. He also felt that France, tied to Bonn and progressively improving its relations with Moscow, was

---

17. For a West German balance sheet twenty years after the Berlin wall, see Juergen Ruehle and Guenther Holzweissig, _13. August 1961: Die Mauer von Berlin_ (Cologne: Edition Deutschland Archiv, 1981), pp. 5-18.

18. Konrad Adenauer, _Erinerrungen, 1955-1959_ (Stuttgart: Deutsche Verlags Anstalt, 1967), pp. 369-396.

19. On the West German debate of the mid-1960s, see Karl Kaiser, _German Foreign Policy in Transition: Bonn Between East and West_ (Oxford: Oxford University Press, 1968), pp. 80-107.

best placed to move this conception gradually forwards. At least since the Soviet-German treaty concluded during the Genoa conference at Rapallo in April 1922, the question of avoiding the joint domination of Europe by Germany and the Soviet Union appears as an over-riding goal for France.[20] Settling Soviet-German differences through French mediation and, to a certain degree, arbitration seemed to be the best guarantee of French long-run security objectives and global aspirations. There would slowly emerge a Europe from the Atlantic to the Urals drawn together by history, culture and national interests, in which Germany was to realize its foreign policy goals, including reunification.[21]

The events in Czechoslovakia seriously checked the French movement towards a rapprochement with the Soviet Union which had reached its most intensive state during de Gaulle's state visit to the Soviet Union in June 1966. After the Soviet intervention in August 1968, the duration, at least for the time being, of a more static model of the European system based on the continuing power of Soviet hegemony was reconfirmed. Moreover, Gaullist policies hastened the day when Germany would begin moving eastwards on its own, without France as broker or mediator, and much less as arbiter. In an apparently paradoxical way, Chancellor Brandt's Ostpolitik, which de Gaulle had been recommending for years, diminished France's influence and rendered more difficult her efforts to remain the favored European interlocutor of the Soviet Union.[22]

Far from ceding to Bonn a role the Germans can play with so much more substance, France has continued to insist on her special status even when the process of "detente, entente and cooperation"[23] failed to live up to de Gaulle's original premises. After 1968, the

---

20. See Renata Bournazel, _Rapallo: naissance d'un mythe. La politique de la peur dans la France du Bloc National_ (Paris: Fondation nationale des sciences politiques, 1974).

21. Press conference of February 4, 1965, _Discours et messages_, vol. 4, p. 341.

22. Alfred Grosser, "Western Europe," in _The Soviet Impact on World Politics_, ed. Kurt L. London (New York: Hawthorn Books, 1974), p. 89.

23. For a Soviet view depicting this Gaullist concept as basically status-quo-oriented, see I.A. Manfred, _Pariž-Bonn: Franko-zapadno-germanskie otnošenija vo vnešnej politike pjatoj respubliki 1958-1968_ (Moscow, Nauka, 1970), p. 149.

French did not abandon the pursuit of national independence but at the same time manifested more reluctance than before to close off their strategic options in calling on Allies to meet commonly perceived exterior threats.24/ President Pompidou, like his predecessor, attempted to strengthen the French bargaining position over a European political settlement by nurturing the Franco-Soviet detente begun in the middle of the 1960s. However, increasing concern about Soviet intentions in Western Europe and Chancellor Brandt's opening to the East reinforced Pompidou's fears of another Rapallo.25/

France had little choice but to back Germany's efforts to improve relations with Eastern Europe,26/ but in the whole complex of negotiations involved in Brandt's Ostpolitik, her major interest had been to insure that any arrangement did not infringe adversely on any rights accruing to the Four-power guarantors. German negotiators and policy-makers were asked with some insistence to safeguard the rights of the Western Allies in Germany--in Berlin in particular--and the French even called upon the British and Americans to back them up in this. Insofar as Ostpolitik weakened the role of the Western Powers in Berlin through the enhanced status of East Germany, Soviet acceptance of co-responsibility for access rights to and from West Berlin as well as of some political, socio-economic and other ties between the Federal Republic and West Berlin, constituted the principal Western negotiating topic in the Four-power Berlin talks. The Berlin Agreement of September 3, 1971 turned out to be relatively satisfactory for France since it presented an opportunity to secure her war-won rights and responsibilities on a more solid foundation and to maintain her claim to participate with the superpowers on equal terms in

---

24. See Ernst Weisenfeld, _Frankreichs Geschichte seit dem Krieg_ (Munich: Beck, 1980), pp. 227-230.

25. According to Kissinger, President Pompidou expressed this fear quite openly in his visit of February 1970 to the United States. See Henry A. Kissinger, _White House Years_ (Boston: Little, Brown, 1979), pp. 422-423.

26. In early July 1970, the final communique after Pompidou's talks in Bonn stated that the Federal Republic has the full backing of France in her attempts to "normalize" her relations with the East. See _Le Monde_, July 7, 1970.

58

settling Germany's future.<u>27</u>/

"The real sovereignty of Berlin was awarded to the victors of World War II" de Gaulle once stressed in a revealing talk with the American journalist Sulzberger.<u>28</u>/   Ten years after de Gaulle's departure from power, President Giscard d'Estaing's visit to West Berlin in October 1979 made clear that the French position with regard to the Berlin problem had not fundamentally altered. Unlike British and American heads of state whose visits to Berlin have always been arranged as part of a state visit to the Federal Republic, the French president chose to fly directly to Berlin from his own country, thus underlining the fact that in his view the quadripartite control over Berlin was not affected by the practical arrangements reached in the Berlin Agreement of September 1971. This sharp reminder of France's status as an occupying power was best summarized in his speech at the Berlin State Library: "Our rights represent your liberty. Our rights represent your security."<u>29</u>/

Forty years after the end of World War II, President Mitterrand decided, however, to take into account the West German bid for more equality in the Franco-German relationship. In the autumn of 1985, the French president will pay a visit to Berlin after a stopover at Bonn-Cologne airport, where Chancellor Kohl joins the French delegation.

As seen from France, Berlin has provided the focus for external interpretations of Ostpolitik and the context by which to measure the degree of compatibility of Ostpolitik with other major power interests and goals in Europe. In the 1950s and the 1960s the Soviet Union tended to view Berlin as a convenient lever for pressure against the West. At the beginning of the 1980s, raising of tensions in Berlin has become counterproductive to Soviet efforts in other areas which the Soviet Union considers more important. The Quadripartite Agreement has brought almost fifteen years of relative stability, but it is still in the Berlin context that Soviet leverage for influence in and over the Federal

---

27. For a detailed account of the Berlin Agreement see Henri Ménudier, "<u>Le règelment</u> de Berlin," in <u>Conflits et coopération entre les Etats</u> (Paris: A. Colin, 1973), pp. 161-188.

28. Cited in Kolodziej, <u>French International Policy under DeGaulle and Pompidou</u>, p. 162.

29. <u>Le Monde</u>, October 30, 1979.

Republic is rooted as well as the Soviet claim to equality with the United States in Europe. The French attitude to the present and future role of Berlin is clearly influenced by the double concern of holding on to the legal responsibilities secured in Berlin and of resisting moves by another power that might dilute France's privileged right to participate as one of the "Big Four" in the decisions about the German "question."

PART TWO

The East

5

West Berlin-GDR Relations:
A West German Perspective

Eberhard Schulz

The future of West Berlin is primarily a German concern. It has been and will remain so for obvious reasons: While the two superpowers and the European nations have, more or less, accommodated themselves to the partition and to living in two separate hegemonial spheres, the German question cannot be settled finally until the condominium of the four Powers in Berlin is superseded by some kind of a normal state order. In other words, there can be no true normalcy until a German rule has been restored in that city, which, for three-quarters of a century, served as the only capital of the German nation-state. In political terms, West Berlin constitutes a strange island surrounded by the territory of a separate state, although both are part of the same German nation. Not only is West Berlin cut off from its traditional hinterland but also from the other half of the city. The frontier even divided families and close personal relationships.

But all of this is only part of the story. Berlin's predicament does not affect the Germans alone and is not solely a Four-power concern. It is not merely conditioned by the East-West rift or by the deficiencies of the East German state. It is also a result of problems created by the emergence of nation-states as basic elements of the political structure of Europe which have profoundly shaken the intra-European balance of power during the last two centuries. These deep-rooted problems as well as their possible implications for future security relations in Europe warrant consideration in the context of the Berlin question. A set of basic premises should therefore be established before the more complex issues surrounding the possible futures of West Berlin and the German Democratic Republic (GDR) can be considered.

FACTORS THAT CONDITION THE STATUS OF WEST BERLIN

First, the postwar occupation and administration of Berlin were a common Four-power endeavor. The Western Powers sought not just to prevent a further expansion of the Soviet Union towards central Europe. They were primarily to control the future development of the German nation which, at the time, constituted the strongest power in central Europe and even now exceeds by far all neighboring nations in population.

Second, the occupation of Berlin followed from World War II and was, therefore, intended and prepared for a transitional period only. No one at the time foresaw the tangle of legal questions that emerged in the course of postwar development. Thus, Berlin and the two incipient German states happened into an increasingly complex international confrontation, and thus provided the fodder for decades of conflict.

Third, since the four (originally three, plus France) Powers had concluded an agreement on a common occupation and administration of Berlin in September 1944, the problem of West Berlin cannot be treated irrespective of the whole city. Many legal provisions still in force pertain to Greater Berlin. There are no legal grounds for exempting East Berlin and applying them only to the western sectors.

Fourth, while, in practical terms, the three Western Powers ensure West Berlin's security, the viability of the city is dependent on political care and financial subsidies from the Federal Republic of Germany. Hence, the connection between the Federal Republic and West Berlin is indispensable.

Fifth, certain asymmetries weigh heavy on the viability of West Berlin: While East Berlin is adjacent to, and indeed included in, the GDR, West Berlin is separated from the FRG by some 180 kilometers of GDR territory and is forbidden by the Quadripartite Agreement to form a constituent part of the FRG (as was ruled by the three Western Powers from the outset). The Western Powers adhered to the provisions of the London Agreement of 1944, while the Soviet Union changed its attitude in order at once to please its German client-state and to enhance its consolidation.

Sixth, the visible occupation status of West Berlin and, to a much less apparent extent, of East Berlin constitutes a symbol of Germany's provisional status. It can be viewed by the Germans as an anchor of hope for an eventual reunification of the nation and thereby serves, to a certain degree, as cement binding the Germans to the Atlantic alliance. At the same time, the prospect of an eventual reunification of the two Germanies is viewed by some of Germany's neighbors, notably the French and the Poles, as a threat to their security. This forms a divisive element within the NATO alliance on the one hand and an incentive to the Poles to maintain an association with the Soviet Union on the other.

Seventh, during the cold war, West Berlin was seen as a spearhead of the free world. In this sense, West Berlin was asked to demonstrate the superiority of the Western way of life in order to counteract the consolidation of the communist German state and the stabilization of Soviet predominance in Eastern Europe. From the viewpoint of the GDR, West Berlin has remained a divisive factor not only because of the large number of human contacts between the two parts of the city, always threatening to politically contaminate East Germany's population, but also because of the impact of broadcasting and television from West Berlin on the population of the GDR.

Finally, West Berlin's viability is, to a certain degree, dependent on a peaceful relationship with the GDR. One need only consider the problems of sewage and garbage, although it can also be argued that Berliners--East and West--share a common fate, since pollution and poisoning of West Berlin would inevitably encroach upon East Berlin and the area around the city. More dangerous political leverage might be provided to the GDR in the field of psychological warfare which, to be sure, can be applied by East Berlin only in accordance with Moscow.

WEST BERLIN AND THE GDR: CHALLENGE OR LEVERAGE?

As a city surrounded by foreign territory, West Berlin is not a singular phenomenon in world history. The most obvious parallel is that of Danzig between the two world wars. But the differences are striking: The municipality of Danzig had played an individual role for centuries. It was situated in an area of ethnic disputes, and the creation of the Free City of Danzig, under the auspices of the League of Nations, in 1920 was meant to be a final solution to a highly explosive issue. Another example might be the Holy See which, like West Berlin, is just a part of the whole city. But, again, the Roman context is hardly comparable. While papal rule is regarded by many in the Roman upper strata as a constant challenge to the secular Italian state, it no longer constitutes a threat, neither militarily nor politically, to the stability of the state and its system. There has in fact developed quite a satisfactory symbiosis of the nation-state and the spiritual authority.

In view of the premises noted above, it is easily understandable why the present GDR leadership is not inclined to accept West Berlin as a permanent political entity. Until the erection of the wall, which eventually closed the last portal to the West for the East German population, Walter Ulbricht time and again tried to persuade Khrushchev unilaterally to attempt to end quadripartite rule in Berlin and to force the Western Powers out of the city.   As a minimum he demanded the conclusion of a separate peace treaty between the Soviet Union and the GDR as well as the transformation of West Berlin into a "Free City" which would deprive it of any reliable and powerful protection and thus sooner or later make it fall victim to the GDR.   It was indicative of Russian second thoughts that they risked the humiliation of the SED (Socialist Unity party of Germany) regime, which in 1961 had to resort to the building of the wall, rather than resign their rights regarding Germany as a whole by abolishing the Four-power status.   As Ulbricht continued to obstruct a compromise even in 1971, the Soviets removed him.

Erich Honecker accepted the compromise of the Quadripartite Agreement, but his subsequent behavior raises serious doubts as to his readiness to keep the _modus vivendi_ and to foreswear all pretensions regarding West Berlin.   In leaving the Berlin question open, he finds himself in agreement with the federal government in Bonn, although for quite different reasons: The Federal Republic of Germany (FRG) wants to keep the German question open because the re-unification of the country is not possible now; the GDR leadership denies the very existence of any German question and just accepts the modus vivendi on Berlin, since its incorporation into the GDR is not feasible at the moment.   But there remains some ambivalence in the sense that Honecker's unwillingness to accept a viable West Berlin which is not part of the territory of the GDR underlines the provisional character of the German situation.   One might argue that this destabilizing factor does exist regardless of the attitude of the GDR as long as the three Western Powers maintain their rights in Germany. One might even argue muting the irredentist claim on West Berlin would be interpreted by the East German population as resignation or weakness of the SED leadership and would therefore involve a certain risk. Yet the fact remains that the termination of uncertainties about the German nation ranks high on the priority list of the communist leaders.

East German Options and Constraints

Any strategy the West might develop for Berlin must inevitably take into account the leverage the GDR has and the incentives or sanctions which the West can bring to bear vis-à-vis the GDR.   The GDR has many choices, but must also live with definite limits on its capability.

Many people in the West are convinced that the GDR's ultimate goal is to swallow West Berlin. They feel that the GDR will be unable to forge a complete internal consolidation as long as the West is in a position to display the superiority of its economic and political system through the window of West Berlin. The East German regime cannot tolerate the ugly symbol of inferiority which the wall constitutes in the most densely populated city, and indeed the capital, of the GDR. Looking down from the restaurant at the top of the TV tower in East Berlin one realizes in a most drastic form how the East Germans are encircled by the wall. The impact of West German television would be sharply reduced if the West Berlin transmitting stations were incorporated into the communist system, although the new epoch of satellite TV is imminent, and it is not at all to be taken for granted that international agreements will be concluded soon to the effect that TV and radio broadcasts have to be confined more or less to the emitting country.

There is another reason which might motivate the East German leadership to strive for an inclusion of West Berlin into the GDR. Unless a final settlement of the German question is reached, the Soviets can insist on their right to interfere in domestic and other affairs of the GDR. It would certainly be an illusion to assume that the Kremlin will abstain from exerting its predominance over the GDR as soon as the Four-power rights formally expire, but a continuation of Soviet hegemony would then be deprived of any legal pretext and could be based only on an agreement with the GDR or on plain force. Even if this did not make much difference in practical terms, an annexation of West Berlin would at least relieve the GDR from its inferior position vis-à-vis its companions in the Warsaw Treaty Organization.

Two more possible reasons might be added. The economic capabilities of the GDR would be considerably expanded if West Berlin were incorporated into the GDR system, and last, but perhaps not least, with the capital of the former German Reich on its territory the GDR would be in a better position to play on national feelings in West Germany and even revive certain dreams which seem to have vanished in the younger and middle generations of Germans. In view of the inherent weakness of the GDR as compared with the FRG, in numbers and in political stability, this might be considered an unacceptable gamble by the SED leadership. Yet some might favor keeping the option open--certainly not in order to eventually reunify the German nation, but to use it to destabilize, in a propitious historic constellation, the FRG and the Western alliance.

Similar strategic considerations might induce the GDR leadership to attempt to undermine the stability of West Berlin. The SEW (Socialist Unity party of West

68

Berlin) is simply an agent of the SED and does not constitute a political factor in West Berlin, attracting only one percent of the electorate. Since it has no chance to win within the parliamentary system, its purpose seems to be to remind the West Berliners of potential future risks. While this crude instrument apparently has no impact on the psychological stability of West Berlin, the GDR seems to apply more subtle means at the same time.

The Special Problem of Demographic Change

One of West Berlin's vulnerabilities is the growing number of foreign minorities, notably Turks and Pakistanis. Large numbers of such immigrants have arrived for some time via the East Berlin airport of Schoenefeld and asked for political asylum in West Berlin. In 1980 certain restrictions were introduced in the FRG (including West Berlin) to prevent foreigners from those countries from settling in the FRG for other than strict political reasons, since it had been discovered that clandestine organizations had developed a real trade with people wanting to emigrate for reasons of personal welfare. The influx of foreigners into West Berlin, however, continued. Within four days in early July 1981, some 600 people, primarily from Sri Lanka, who arrived via Schoenefeld, had asked for political asylum. Exact figures are not available, since immigrants passing through the GDR under legal procedures are not controlled when entering West Berlin, because the Basic Law of the FRG, applicable also in West Berlin, provides for free movement inside Germany (including the GDR). It is up to the East German authorities, therefore, to decide how many foreigners to channel into West Berlin. To avoid deportation, the illegal immigrants do not register. Most of them live under ghetto-like conditions, which lead to an explosive accumulation of tensions. The FRG and the West Berlin Senate had been negotiating with the GDR for years about restricting unauthorized entry from Asia. Finally, the GDR airline Interflug announced that by July 15, 1985, no passengers would be transported to Schoenefeld without a valid visa for the GDR or the FRG. The Soviet airline Aeroflot followed suit. Yet it remains to be seen whether excessive immigration can now be barred.

As early as the 1940s, the communists tried to stir irritation with the Berliners against the three Western Powers. This was a futile endeavor. Fear of the Russians overshadowed all other feelings with the population, and American "raisin bombers," as Berliners gratefully called the relief planes during the airlift in 1948-1949, gave visible proof of the fact that freedom was protected by the Western occupation forces.

Later Berlin crises reinforced this basic experience. However, a gradual change in attitudes began during the era of detente. In the early 1970s many Berliners distrusted any attempt to reach accommodation with the East, which they felt might eventually compromise their security. Soon, however, the process of normalization vis-à-vis East Berlin led the younger generation to begin to doubt the need for Western military presence. Certain inconveniences and, at least partly unavoidable, disadvantages such as military maneuvers in the main recreation area of Grunewald caught the attention of people concerned with environment damage and not experienced in the hardships of armed conflicts. GDR propaganda eagerly exploited emotions and psychological wavering whenever they occurred.

One point, often overlooked, warrants attention. Anybody in the Federal Republic as well as in West Berlin is aware of the necessity for the FRG to provide economic and financial assistance for the insular city. Neither the federal Minister of Finance nor the Bundestag have ever raised difficulties or uttered objections against the Berlin assistance act. But few people have ever asked whether this high degree of insulation of West Berlin from the GDR must be an inevitable fate forever. It is obviously in the interest of the GDR to strengthen the impression that precisely this is the case. There is no indication whatever, for the time being, that the GDR is inclined to lessen its pressure, which is one of the most important reasons for the exodus of so many Berliners to the FRG. The GDR leadership may hope that this migration will lead to a situation when West Berlin is "ripe" (to put it in Leninist terms) for a communist takeover. Aspirations for destabilizing and eventually even swallowing West Berlin are not necessarily incompatible with a strategy that leaves both alternative options open--the incorporation as well as the peaceful neighborhood. At any rate, the GDR leadership has to maintain its present modus vivendi simply because the Kremlin has so ordered. Whatever objections may be raised against this policy, even the hawks in East Berlin have to admit that no other policy offers more leverage against the FRG. The communication lines between Berlin and West Germany are an opulent source of hard currency and West German finance contributes, at the same time, to an improvement of the East German infrastructure. However, in case of political turbulence the West Germans need to protect the viability, notably the psychological stability, of West Berlin.

With respect to domestic stability, a cautious attitude towards West Berlin is probably in order. On the one hand, the East Germans are aware of the sensitivity of the Berlin problem. They want to live in peace and not to compromise their achievements, modest as they are, by an adventurous policy. On the other hand, the SED leadership is only now beginning to develop normal relationships with Western governments, which did not rush to exchange high level visits with GDR officials after extending recognition in the 1970s. Any precipitous policy of the Soviet bloc against West Berlin would deprive the SED leaders of the fruits of their strenuous and patient efforts to gain international respectability.

Theoretically, the GDR leadership might opt not just to maintain a modus vivendi with West Berlin, but cautiously to develop a constructive policy such as the strategy the Chinese have used so profitably vis-à-vis Hong Kong. They might greatly expand economic relations by exploiting the extensive West Berlin infrastructure and the rich expertise of West Berlin's service business. They might expand their import of manufactured goods (beyond the technology they so avidly seek) This trade has been at an extremely low level for years in sharp defiance of rational economic considerations. This would enhance the competitive capacity of West Berlin's business, which lags behind now as a consequence of reduced competition in a very narrow market. Yet the GDR economy would clearly benefit from the low transportation costs. Additional profit could be drawn from the outstanding West Berlin capacity for research and development. Little has been done in this field to this point.

It is difficult to assess the real intentions of the GDR leadership. Any predictions about the future behavior of the East Germans remain highly speculative. Yet systematic research isolate the criteria which determine the decisions of the GDR leadership. Their past performance clearly indicates that the East German leaders see the maintenance of their own power as their foremost priority. To this end they need three important elements, namely a minimum of loyalty of the population, a properly functioning administration, and the backing of the Kremlin leadership.

The loyalty of the GDR population depends greatly on satisfactory economic and social development. It would be endangered by an adventurous policy implying the risk of an armed conflict. Any possible options toward West Berlin must be more or less compatible with the people's socio-economic demands; there is no strong pressure for good, neighborly relations. The same is true for political-military relations--except during an acute crisis. The second element, a functioning administration, is not affected by any Berlin policy. The remaining factor is the predominant political trend in the Kremlin. It will be influenced by the prevailing circumstances, although one is on the safe side guessing that the Russians will not enter a major risk just for the sake of Berlin, and that they will always try to keep their finger in the German pie and not let the East Germans slip from their hand. Since a retreat of the Western Powers from Berlin would blur the legal claims of the Four altogether, it is not very likely that the Soviets will force the Western Powers out. They would simply endanger their own position in Germany as a whole and vis-à-vis the GDR. Thus, all of the options remain possible, provided European security is not endangered. Which the East German leaders will choose depends on their assessment of the respective benefits and risks and, of course, on Soviet consent.

PSYCHOLOGICAL FACTORS IN WEST BERLIN:
DESPAIR, HOPES, DISILLUSION

Although Joseph Goebbels predicted in the waning months of World War II that the Allied Powers, when victorious, would wipe out the German Reich, in the immediate postwar period few Germans could really imagine a German state with a capital other than Berlin. While most people simply were exhausted when this total war had come to an end, those politically active anti-Nazis who had remained in, or had come back to, Berlin tried to save as much of the Reich as seemed feasible. Even "Ulbricht's group," a team of German communists sent to Berlin by Stalin from their exile in the Soviet Union, aimed at restoring a German republic with their headquarters in the heavily destroyed capital of Berlin. And, interestingly, they then explicitly declined the Oder-Neisse line as the German frontier with Poland.

The desperate mood of the majority of the starving people contrasted sharply with the hopes of the active forces of all parts of the political spectrum who began to reorganize a democratic political life. Even the administration of the Soviet sector shortly after the war entrusted "bourgeois" personalities with certain responsibilities. Conservative and liberal politicians recalled German (or Prussian)-Russian cooperation with the tsarist dynasty of the Romanovs or even with Lenin and his successors after "Rapallo." Prominent leaders of the Christian Democratic and the Liberal parties tried to compromise with Soviet authorities in order to convince them of their peaceful intentions and thus preserve at least some independence for the German population. Some Social Democrats mindful of the common persecution of communists and SPD members in the Nazi concentration camps hoped to repair the split of the workers' movement, which had allowed Hitler to seize power. Hoping to outnumber the communists, many Berlin Social Democrats agreed to the merger of SPD and the Communist party of Germany (KPD), forming the Socialist Unity party of Germany (SED), in defiance of the sharp objection raised by their West German party leader Kurt

Schumacher. To a certain degree these forces felt justified when they knew that the first resistance against the installation of central German adminis- trative agencies under occupation rule, as agreed to by the Potsdam conference, was voiced by the French government. In 1945-1946 it was by no means clear that the victorious Powers in East and West would eventually approve some kind of German statehood again.

But Soviet tolerance of democratic structures in their occupation zone very soon proved limited in scope and time. Communist forces pressed for preparation for the "socialist transformation" of the society. In view of the fact that the living standards even in the defeated Germany were much higher than in the Soviet Union, the Soviet leadership indiscriminately dismantled industrial installations, including critical infrastruc- ture such as railway lines. Mutual distrust grew between East and West. Its roots lay in the conduct of the war itself. Stalin suspected that the Americans deliberately had delayed their invasion of France in 1944 in order to weaken the Soviets in their fighting against the Germans and eventually to destroy the Soviet system after the victory over Hitler. These and other conflicts finally erupted in the cold war. The communist coup in Prague in February 1948, came as a shock to Western publics. In the meantime an open struggle had begun for power in the city parliament of Berlin in which Soviet authorities interfered heavily. The freely elected mayor was prevented from fulfilling his obligations, and eventually the magistrate was expelled from the city hall, located in the Soviet sector. The legal authorities moved into the American sector. Some months before, the Soviet member of the Allied Kommandatura had boycotted the work of this supreme administration. The first phase of the division of Berlin had been completed. Berliners now endured a new and unexpected set of pressures.

The next phase of Berlin's history was marked by increasing attractiveness of the Western sectors. After the Soviet attempt to enforce their will on the whole city by blockading the Western sectors had failed thanks to Western toughness and the Anglo-American airlift, the European Recovery Program financed impressive economic growth in West Germany and West Berlin. The reconstruc- tion of the Western sectors made quick progress. The center, including the modernist Hansa quarter shaped by renowned international architects, and the lights of the "Kudamm" became a symbol of Western well-being. As West Berliners became more proud of their advancing city and enjoyed their democratic system, opposition within the East German state grew stronger. This sometimes resulted in armed assaults on communist installations, since many people did not want a second dictatorship to be estab- lished in Germany. Traffic across the transit lines between the Federal Republic of Germany and West Berlin was more or less normal. West Berliners and West Germans visit East Berlin, and East Berliners freely traveled west. Hence, the higher living standards in the West became very salient for East Germans. Western radio (and later television) broadcasts covered nearly all of the GDR in its native language. Thus West Berlin became the show window of the West, and West Berlin's self-assurance grew accordingly.

Ominous clouds appeared on West Berlin's horizon when in 1958 Khrushchev announced his ultimatum. People slowly began to realize that they were at risk. The former capital was detached from its country. There was no large government apparatus anymore, save for a few second-rank agencies. The ministries of the federal government had been established, if on a temporary basis, in Bonn. Interest groups of trade and industry, as well as the unions, and even the big corporations had moved their headquarters to Bonn early on, leaving a secondary presence, at best, in Berlin. This was not extremely embarrassing as long as there was a constant flow of refugees from the GDR who made use of the only remaining exit from the East German state. The newcomers always filled the gap of manpower during this period of rapid economic growth. But then, in 1961, the wall was built.

The construction of the wall shocked not only the East Germans, who finally lost the possibility of escaping the communist system without risking their lives. It also hit West Berlin very hard. It was not just the sudden manpower problem. There was a very deep crisis of confidence in West German and Western solidarity. This time the Americans did not help. Their tanks stopped at Checkpoint Charlie and did not impede Ulbricht's activities. Federal Chancellor Konrad Adenauer needed several weeks to get to Berlin. He made it plain that all contingency planning of the West did not help in a situation when there was no direct armed conflict, and that the viability of West Berlin was questionable not only in the case of a war.

It was Willy Brandt, West Berlin's mayor since 1957, who realized first the turn in the political development of the divided city. He recognized the need for a policy of detente vis-à-vis the GDR in order to maintain the political existence of West Berlin. Economic prosperity remained, but there was also growing nervousness in the population. For the first time since the blockade of 1948-1949, psychological factors became paramount in West Berlin.

For the Federal Republic and for the West in general, notably in their stance towards the East German state, the city had become a liability rather than an asset, as Bonn maintained that the GDR continued to be the Soviet zone of occupation in Germany and lacked any legitimacy to be recognized by the Western democracies as an independent state. The GDR, on the other hand, used pressure against West Berlin and its access routes as a lever in order to overcome West German opposition to its international recognition.

By historical coincidence the modern age of West German terrorism was born in Berlin. In June 1967, a student was shot by a fearful West Berlin policeman during a demonstration against the brutal behavior of Iranian security forces. This led to the founding of a terrorist group which called itself the "Second of June Movement." But it was not at all a coincidence that the wave of dissatisfaction with the two big parties which formed a grand coalition in Bonn (thus precluding effective parliamentary opposition) reached its peak in West Berlin. It was in this city that the lack of momentum, flexibility, and imagination which characterized the policy of the Bonn establishment vis-à-vis the GDR, was sensed most clearly and provoked the gathering of rather diffuse forces which became known as "extra-parliamentary opposition"--the only common denominator of which was the loss of confidence in the main political parties. One of their outstanding demands was the turn from empty wording about "unity in freedom" for the German nation to concrete activities in order to improve, and indeed revive, personal contacts between the people in the East and West of the divided country.

This was precisely what Willy Brandt immediately sought when he was elected Chancellor in 1969. But very soon it became apparent that he had run into a dilemma as far as Berlin was concerned. Any reconciliation with the East European countries inevitably implied abandonment or at least qualification of some of Bonn's traditional legal positions. This was welcomed by large parts of West Berlin's intelligentsia. Other groups, however, had grave doubts. For example, the middle class, in line with the CDU opposition, viewed accommodation with the East at best as a lack of professional expertise and moral weakness and at worst even as proclivity towards "self-finlandization" or of yielding to Soviet blackmail. This view was widely shared and produced a deep-rooted insecurity when the treaties with Moscow, Warsaw, East Berlin, and Prague were signed. It was a tragic irony of history that the only treaty which was not negotiated by the Germans themselves, but contributed most to alleviating the difficulties between the two separated parts of Berlin, the Quadripartite Agreement, caused the greatest anxiety among the population of West Berlin. The treaty evoked strong emotions in West Berlin, caused by the traumas of 1948-1949 and of 1961. Irrational fears and reactions seemed impervious to logical explanation.

Any policy pursued by the FRG toward the GDR and the Soviet Union henceforth had to take into account psychological factors in West Berlin. Berliners had three basic concerns: First, they felt exposed to Soviet piecemeal tactics, which had been applied by Moscow so often in the past. People remembered the fate of the three Baltic nations in 1940, the removal under poor pretext of noncommunist antifascist personalities in East Berlin and in the Soviet occupation zone after 1945, the overthrow of the democratic system in Prague in 1948, the interference with the access routes through the GDR, and many other similar events.

Second, there were the doubts that inevitably arose from West Berlin's geographic separation from the Federal Republic by some 180 kilometers of GDR territory. Cut off from its hinterland, West Berlin was not viable on its own. It had to be subsidized by the West Germans as long as the sharp antagonism between the two global systems persisted and prevented the establishment of normal relations with the GDR. But are the West Germans really reliable? Didn't they shift from using West Berlin as their favorite show window against the GDR during the cold war to talking about neighborly relations between the two German states? How would the existence of West Berlin and its dependence on the FRG fit into this picture of avoiding provocations against the communist German state? Wouldn't Soviet military preponderance in Europe and the employment of West German workers to produce steel pipes for the Soviet Union urge Bonn to keep a low profile in case of Soviet blackmail against West Berlin? Wasn't it true that the policy of detente corresponded to Soviet demands, and didn't the world experience the consequences of French and British appeasement of Nazi Germany? To be sure, there are no easy answers to gnawing doubts like these, and it is hard to imagine that irrational, and to some extent indeed very rational, anxieties might be dissipated by the simple question of what different policy might offer a more stable guarantee or whether there is any policy Bonn might pursue creating absolute security in view of West Berlin's peculiar situation. The fact that the Berlin policy of the West until 1969 failed to provide a stable solution provides no consolation.

Many West Berliners, therefore came to the third conclusion, namely that it is only a matter of time until the GDR will consume the whole of the city, the eastern part of which it already calls "Berlin, the capital of the GDR" without any regard for international law. East German officials have long claimed that West Berlin was situated "on the territory of the GDR." The complicated situation of West Berlin resulted in a persistent brain and business drain to West Germany. The former German capital suffered shortages of ambitious and intelligent personnel in business and administration, people badly needed to tackle the countless

76

complex problems of the city. Without offering a
brighter future there is little hope of filling these
personnel gaps. In practical terms this means it is
necessary to break the mentality of isolation in West
Berlin and to convince the GDR leadership that in their
own difficult situation, it is in their best interest to
overcome their hostile attitude toward West Berlin.
This is admittedly not an easy task under present conditions.

OPTIONS AND PROSPECTS FOR RELATIONS WITH THE GDR

In terms of the basic premises noted at the outset
of this chapter, West Berlin's changing roles in East-
West relations during the last three and one-half
decades, and the psychological vulnerability of the
Berliners in their remote position, it is easy to define
the tasks Bonn has to fulfill in its policy toward the
GDR and the Soviet Union. And to fully maintain the
viability of West Berlin, of course, Bonn must define a
policy that also is compatible with its relationship
with the three Western Powers, the European Community,
and the Atlantic alliance. The real difficulty begins
when the optimal policy is to be chosen.
The declared purpose of official German _Deutsch-
landpolitik_ is "to aim at a state of peace in Europe in
which the German nation regains its unity by means of
free self-determination." Such a state of affairs is
obviously far away, and it is impossible now to develop
a concrete strategy for its achievement. This does not
mean, however, that a German government acting in a
responsible way is allowed to lose sight of the whole
complex of problems involved, because the prospects of
Berlin are inseparably intertwined with essential
security interests of the European nations. That means
that the government of the FRG has to consider the
compatibility of any step it undertakes in its policy
vis-à-vis Berlin and the GDR, with the development of an
overall peaceful structure in central Europe. The forms
in which the unity of the German nation may be regained
in an historical era which might be called a "post-
nation-state era" are open to discussion. Supranational
integration processes, though still incremental,
indicate perspectives of hitherto unknown solutions. It
is in this context that the merits of practical short
and medium-term initiatives regarding Berlin and the GDR
should be evaluated.
The primary medium-term objective Bonn has to bear
in mind is the perpetuation of the Four-power responsibilities concerning Berlin and Germany as a whole.
They not only form the best kind of guarantee for
stability in and around West Berlin, but also may lead
some day, when East-West antagonism has subsided, to an

effective all-European security system in which there is no need to split the German nation by artificial and cruel barriers. In the short run it is essential for the viability of West Berlin to keep the three Western Powers committed to Berlin. There was a time in the 1950s and 1960s when the Bonn government felt it advisable to use every opportunity to appeal to the moral obligation and the mercy of the three Allies. Reminding the three Powers, when necessary, that the Soviets are impressed by toughness, and that the victorious Powers occupied Berlin in 1945 in view of the stake they have in Germany, might better serve the purpose.

It is equally important to preclude any weakening of the substantial ties between West Berlin and the Federal Republic. As long as the GDR behaves in a hostile manner against West Berlin, the city is dependent on transfusions from the FRG. This will likely endure for some time, even if the East German leaders recognize the advantages normal relations with West Berlin might offer them in economic as well as in political terms. But in the longer run a substantial improvement of the relations between the GDR and West Berlin should not be considered totally unrealistic. Only when the GDR has changed its attitude towards West Berlin and has developed genuinely good relations will West Berlin may become largely viable on its own. In the meantime the Federal Republic will continue negotiating with the GDR in order at least to alleviate bureaucratic procedures impeding communications between West Berlin and its surroundings as well as transit to the FRG.

The future development of West Berlin's relations with the GDR, as far as it can be influenced by the Federal Republic of Germany, largely depends on the objectives Bonn brings into focus. Theoretically, one might discern four basic options:

First, Bonn might proceed on the assumption that the final goal of restoring a German nation-state is paramount and that one has to stick to the legal and political position that Berlin still is the capital of the German state and will remain so in the future. In this context Berlin is regarded as the symbol of German unity. Any compromise of this idea would weaken the allegiance of the Germans to their national unity. In a critical moment, which might arise in an economic depression, such as in the early 1930s, a nationalist demagogue might usurp national ideals abandoned by the established democratic parties and exploit them to destroy our greatest postwar achievement--our free democratic system.

This policy also affects the psychological situation in West Berlin. Physically truncated from the rest of the nation, the rationale for its existence is its ideal function of being the German capital. Depriving the Berliners of this hope would definitely demoralize them. As the communists never explicitly rejected the idea of the Germans forming one nation, by neglecting the notion that Berlin constitutes the capital, the West might provide the East with an attractive asset in the struggle for power in Germany.

This opinion, which has been shared more or less explicitly by all governments in Bonn during the past three decades, allows easy rejection of an commonly cited danger: namely that the claim Berlin should again become the capital of a unified German state, makes the very existence of West Berlin unacceptable to the authorities in East Berlin. Indeed, the communists are probably determined to seize West Berlin anyway and any hope to make them compromise is illusionary. Attempts to come to terms with them would even stimulate their appetite. It is therefore necessary to keep the awareness of the threat alive with West Berliners. As long as they are conscious of the nature of communism, they will be resolved to resist any pressure and psychological warfare from the East. The fact that the number of ethnic German West Berliners has declined for years is mainly due to lack of confidence in a Bonn government that promised more security through detente and fell victim to Soviet propaganda while the Kremlin started a potent arms buildup in order to shift the "correlation of forces" to its favor. As no change is in sight, subsidies from Bonn must be increased as part of the Western defense posture.

The second option is quite similar to the first one in motivation as well as in effect. It might even be seenas a corollary of the first one. Its core constitutes the resolve to maximize not only the ties between West Germany and West Berlin but also the presence of FRG institutions in West Berlin, in order to make visible that Berlin is part of the FRG according to the constitutions of the FRG and of the Land of Berlin (which de facto is confined to West Berlin). Only this consciousness provides sufficient guarantee to the German nation and especially to West Berliners that the West Germans will never abandon Berlin. This will at the same time reassure the East German population that the wish for reunification in West Germany is still alive and that the East Germans (or the "intermediate Germans" as they are often called as opposed to the "East Germans" living now under Polish or Soviet administration) should persevere in their opposition to partition until Soviet predominance disappears and the communist regime in the GDR breaks down.

Such a federal German presence in Berlin is in full accord with the Quadripartite Agreement of 1971 and Allied legislation. This is so for two reasons: The three Western Powers vetoed inclusion of the Land of

Berlin into the FRG. However, the Constitutional Court of the FRG has ruled that the veto only suspends, not annuls, the relevant sections of the Basic Law of the FRG and of the constitution of the Land of Berlin. Second, the Quadripartite Agreement states "that the ties between the Western Sectors of Berlin and the Federal Republic of Germany will be maintained and developed, taking into account that these Sectors continue not to be a constituent part of the Federal Republic of Germany and not to be governed by it." Proponents of this option do not acknowledge that this formulation constitutes the expression of a fundamental difference of opinions between the Western Powers on the one hand and the Soviet Union on the other. Hence, Bonn sought shortly after the agreement to test its operation in practice. The Federal Agency for Environmental Protection was established in West Berlin. The Soviet Union objected strongly. This again was regarded as evidence of Soviet abrogation of the terms of the Quadripartite Agreement and prompted demands for more toughness on the Western side. Soviet threats fueled the anxiety of the West Berlin population and strengthened support for a government that takes a stronger stance vis-à-vis the communists.

The third option stresses the importance of West Berlin's independence from the GDR. At present West Berlin's exports to CMEA countries, including the GDR, are small. Imports are higher, because they offer the communist countries hard currency earnings in conjunction with low transportation costs. But the Berlin Senate and the government in Bonn (which oversees intra-German and foreign trade) are anxious to prevent West Berlin from becoming dependent on essential goods from the East. To this end, West Berlin businessmen must be granted compensation for their higher transport costs in form of direct subvention or reduction in taxation. This recommendation stems not only from Western concerns, but also as a response to the policy of confrontation exercised by the GDR and the Soviet Union.

When the present tide of intense antagonism has subsided, and if economic difficulties make governments in East and West more anxious to look for relief from financial burdens, the time may come for a fourth option. It might aim at exchanging mutual benefits rather than creating difficulties for each other. In such circumstances the GDR leadership might lessen its pressure on West Berlin, and the federal government might try to reduce East German opposition to an independent and flourishing West Berlin.

Should the GDR demonstrate such accommodation, Bonn might reconsider its claim that West Berlin remains the legal capital of Germany. Clearly, the German nation might freely decide in favor of a confederation instead of a unified state. The question of a single capital for Germany would then be rendered moot. Bonn might be reassured in discussing such an idea by the obvious fact that this form of the unity of the German nation might be more acceptable also to our Western Allies, notably to the member states of the European Community. Under these circumstances Bonn would also lose any incentive to expand its visible presence in West Berlin.

It goes without saying that certain risks are implied in such an endeavor. The GDR might revert to confrontation and blackmail. It would therefore be necessary to introduce effective precautions. It would also be difficult to mute the apprehensions of West Berliners who so often had to bear the burden of East-West confrontation, and it would be very unwise to underestimate destabilizing psychological factors in West Berlin.

West Berlin cannot be made viable on its own in the long run unless the perception of dependence on West German subsidies is removed. To this end it is worthwhile trying to reach a set of economic accords with the GDR that would aid the West Berlin economy while increasing consumer satisfaction within the East German population. On the international level, of course, the responsibilities of the Four Powers must be maintained, and some sort of closer ties with the FRG, perhaps in the form of a confederation that maintains the occupation status of Berlin, must be established.

The possible mutual benefits of this kind reform should not be underestimated. If not threatened by domestic instability, the GDR might expand its vacation facilities. This would open new choices for leisure to West Berliners and add to hard currency earnings of the GDR. West Berlin has a very efficient industrial potential and valuable research and development installations that could easily service possible customers in the GDR. Such firms might become important trade partners of the GDR.

Unfortunately, while there is much room for imagination, at present prospects do not appear good for a shift from confrontation to mutual beneficial cooperation. But in course of time it might become more difficult for the East to puruse a policy of unequivocal confrontation. As detente ascended in 1970 and 1971, Walter Ulbricht tried to defy Soviet accommodation with the Bonn at the expense of the GDR. He was removed. In 1983 and 1984 his successor Erich Honecker met with popular resistance to increasingly belligerent Soviet policy. Hence, he sought to mediate between Moscow and Bonn. He even took a less hostile attitude toward West Berlin than did Soviet propaganda. Hungary's Kadar backed him quite openly and most other East European leaders maintained a kind of benevolent neutrality. Eventually Honecker was rebuffed by Moscow, but for the time being he survived. Perhaps Mikhail Gorbachev, the new First Secretary of the CPSU, can be convinced that the Soviet Union fares better by muting its position on Berlin. As long as Soviet policy in this area is confined to rhetoric, all options remain open.

6

The Relations Between West Berlin and the Warsaw Pact States

Gerhard Wettig

THE GENESIS OF THE BERLIN PROBLEM

The basic fact determining the relationship between West Berlin and the Eastern countries is that this city is a Western exclave in Warsaw Pact territory. Whenever open East-West conflict has surfaced, the Soviet leadership has tried to make use of West Berlin's vulnerability against the Western Powers. Since the Berlin blockade of 1948-1949, the USSR has repeatedly employed restrictive measures against Western (including West German) access to West Berlin as a tool of pressure and/or threat. Consequently, the Berlin problem became a focus of East-West tension which has produced several crises and even seemed to imply the danger of war. When, in 1969-1970, East and West decided in favor of detente, in order to preclude the risky possibility of mutual crisis and war, there was a strong need to settle the conflicts in Berlin.

The character of the problem has altered since the principal set of serious Berlin crises from 1958 to 1962. The division of Greater Berlin in 1948 had induced each side to link its respective fragment of the city to the other German territory within its power sphere. Accordingly, West Berlin was tied to the Federal Republic of Germany under certain legal reservations. Until 1958, neither the USSR nor the German Democratic Republic (GDR) saw any reason to protest this state of affairs. At that time it was exclusively the Berlin presence of the three Western Powers which they resented. When, however, Khrushchev pushed hard in 1958-1959, he soon discovered that he did not possess sufficient strength to dislodge the Western Powers from West Berlin. Again and again he had to reduce his pressure. In order to save face, Khrushchev felt he had to find a weaker target than the United States. He chose the Federal Republic of Germany. It is in this context that the ties of West Berlin to West Germany developed to be the primary target of Eastern polemics and Eastern attacks. In the 1960s, the USSR increasingly posed as defender of West Berlin's status against West German encroachments—with the obvious benefit that it avoided direct confrontation with the Western Powers (i.e., the United States).1/

Moscow's changed political strategy did not mean that pressure against Western access was dropped. On the contrary, alleged West German violations of West Berlin's status were being used as justifying arguments for gradual restrictive measures which the Eastern propaganda presented as necessary reprisals and as attempts to restore justice. Public Soviet statements even indicated that the USSR defended Western occupation rights against Bonn's disregard for them. In fact, however, Soviet policies (which were followed by the other Warsaw Pact countries with the partial exception of Rumania) went in the opposite direction: Moscow's affirmations that West Berlin's ties to the Federal Republic were illegal rested solely on the assumption that the three Western Powers had no right whatsoever to allow such ties, as their occupation competences were subject to an obligatory consensus with the USSR as the holder of supreme occupational authority in West Berlin.2/ If that claim were acknowledged, the city was bound to be dependent on Soviet goodwill. At the same time it was clear that the existence of West Berlin both economically and politically rested on the availability of the ties to the Federal Republic which the Soviet Union, supported by the Warsaw Pact, sought to destroy.

In 1969-1970, the United States and the USSR agreed to negotiate on the problems which had made Berlin an area of tension and crisis. Both sides held opposing views of how to pacify the situation. On the one hand, Moscow wanted West Berlin to be stripped of its ties to West Germany. Under this condition, the city would no longer be a focus of tension.3/ The three Western

---

1. For details see Gerhard Wettig, Das Vier-Maechte-Abkommen in der Bewaehrungsprobe: Berlin im Spannungsfeld von Ost und West (Berlin: Berlin Verlag, 1981), pp. 73-77.

2. Cf., for example, V.N. Vysotzkii (pseudonym for V.N. Beletskii), Zapadnyi Berlin i ego mesto v sisteme sovremennykh mezhdunarodnykh otnoshenii (Moscow: Mysl', 1971), pp. 330-344. This book is virtually identical to a habilitation thesis submitted to the Institute for International Relations at Akademie fuer Staats- und Rechtswissenschaften, "Walter Ulbricht" in Potsdam-Babelsberg on July 1, 1968.

3. Speech by Soviet Foreign Minister Gromyko before the

Powers, on the other hand, felt that the Soviet Union had to recognize both free Western access to the city and the most basic of the ties established since 1949. Acceptance of the ties, it is true, did not seem to be a legal requirement. The three Western governments felt that they had rights of their own in West Berlin and therefore did not depend on Soviet assent. Soviet acceptance was, however, regarded as politically indispensable so as to prevent further pretext for Eastern restrictive measures at the access routes. The Soviet leaders wanted to avoid just this.

The outcome of the negotiations, the Quadripartite Agreement of September 3, 1971, corresponds largely to the Western view. It provides for "unimpeded" traffic between West Berlin and West Germany which is to "take place in the most simple and expeditious manner" and to "receive preferential treatment." At the same time, "the ties between the Western sectors of Berlin and the Federal Republic of Germany" are to "be maintained and developed, taking into account that these sectors continue not to be a constituent part of the Federal Republic of Germany and not to be governed by it."4/

However, basic political viewpoints and fundamental legal interpretations remained controversial. There was particularly no consensus as to whether the traffic between West Berlin and West Germany was based on Western original right or on GDR sovereign acceptance.5/ Similarly, both sides disagreed on the question of Western competence to allow ties between West Berlin and the Federal Republic6/ and on the nature of those ties (which, in Soviet interpretation, are but quasi-technical connections and imply a status of political separateness for the city).7/

Supreme Soviet on July 10, 1969. _Pravda_, July 11, 1969.

4. _Das Viermaechte-Abkommen ueber Berlin vom 3. September 1971_ (Bonn: Press and Information Office, Federal Republic of Germany, 1971), pp. 179-198.

5. For the Soviet view see, for example, V.N. Vysotskii, _Zapadnyi Berlin_, pp. 291-292, 330-344, 351-360, 362-369, and 413.

6. For the Soviet view see, for example, ibid., pp. 365, and 421-422; and J. Rschewski, _Westberlin--ein Gebilde sui generis_ (Moscow, 1966-1967), pp. 7-29 and 37-51.

7. For the Soviet view see ibid., pp. 30, 33-34, 51-65, 78-79, and 87-88; and V.N. Vysotskii, _Zapadnyi Berlin_, pp. 369-375.

THE BASIC LEGAL DIFFERENCES OVER BERLIN

Open conflict over Berlin has been limited since the Quadripartite Agreement was put into effect early in June 1972. Latent conflict, however, has always been present. It is only mutual restraint largely exercised by both sides which has prevented latent conflict from resulting in severe tension. The potential for conflict lies mainly in the opposing views regarding the status of Berlin. In this respect, the Quadripartite Agreement has totally failed to produce any consensus. The contracting parties have agreed to disagree by expressly stating that they were acting "without prejudice to their legal positions" and exclusively on "the desire to contribute to practical improvements of the situation."

The three Western Powers take the legal view that they have occupied Berlin together with the Soviet Union on an equal basis of original right. It follows from this position:

1. that there is an original Western right of presence in Berlin;

2. that a corresponding right of access to Berlin can be postulated;

3. that after Soviet withdrawal from the inter-Allied Kommandatura a tripartite occupational rule over the Western sectors is the logical consequence;

4. that the USSR cannot unilaterally hand its sector over to the GDR and that, therefore, East Berlin is still under the quadripartite status established in 1945;

5. that the Western original rights have priority over the competences of the GDR (which has come into existence only after the specialties of the Berlin situation had been created) and that accordingly the East German state has to respect unconditionally all its obligations vis-à-vis West Berlin.

These legal interpretations are violently attacked by the USSR. During 1948 and 1949, and consistently since 1958, Moscow has asserted that Berlin has never been anything else but part of the Soviet Occupation Zone. Allegedly, the USSR has but freely conceded limited rights of residence in the Western Sectors to the Western Powers which, however, were made conditional upon acknowledgement of Soviet supreme authority.8/ This legal view has no basis in the fundamental Allied agreements on Berlin reached in 1944-1945 and also cannot be traced in the implementation of those agreements during the subsequent period of quadripartite cooperation in

---

8. Cf. ibid., pp. 330-344 and 421-422.

Germany.<u>9</u>/
Nevertheless, Moscow acts on its thesis as if it were a well established and universally acknowledged fact. The practical consequences are far-reaching:
1.   The existence of an original Western right of presence in Berlin is disclaimed in principle. It is only for reasons of political expediency that the USSR at present--in contrast to 1948-1949 and 1958-1962-- tolerates Western troops and Western authorities in West Berlin.
2.   In the Soviet view, there are no Western access rights. Instead, transit is voluntarily granted. The responsibility for military transit rests with the USSR, while the competence for civilian transit has been transferred to the GDR.
3.   The USSR as the exclusive holder of full occupational authority in Berlin has legitimately turned over its rights regarding the Soviet sector to the GDR. For this reason the quadripartite status now pertains only to West Berlin. The "relevant area" to which the Quadripartite Agreement addresses itself does not include East Berlin (as the Western Powers claim).
4.   Being a quadripartite territory unilaterally, West Berlin is unilaterally subjected to quadripartite rule--a state of affairs which follows from the supreme authority which the USSR claims to have possessed over all of Berlin from the very beginning. Therefore, Moscow regards Western basic decisions over West Berlin as both illegal and invalid, unless they are agreed to by the Soviet Union. This applies in particular to West Berlin's ties to the Federal Republic, the kind and extent of which cannot be determined by the Western Powers. The Soviet standpoint that West Berlin must be a "separate political entity" has always to be taken into full account, and Soviet assent has to be confirmed before any relevant action may be taken.
5.   As a consequence, the Quadripartite Agreement has to be interpreted restrictively: Only what the USSR has expressly "permitted" in the Agreement can be accepted as legally justified; issues not regulated by the contractual consensus reached in 1971, must be regarded as open and can be resolved only with Soviet assent.
6.   As the Western Powers are said to have no claim against the Eastern side in their own right, they

---

9. Cf. Wettig, <u>Das Vier-Maechte-Abkommen</u>, pp. 14-17. Occasional attempts of the Soviet Union to impose uni- lateral measures on the Western partners cannot justify the claim (as Soviet authors try to do)--all the more so, as such measures were effectively counteracted by the Western Powers.

are not seen to be in a privileged situation vis-à-vis the GDR which, in this respect, can claim unlimited sovereignty. The latent implication of this is that in cases of conflict the East German interests legitimately take precedence over Western complaints regarding transit traffic and travel regulations.10/

BRIDGING THE LEGAL DIFFERENCES THROUGH THE
LOGIC OF MODUS VIVENDI

Any of these legal differences (none of which has been diminished by the Quadripartite Agreement) carries the potential for major political conflict. Either side that might feel inclined to adopt a policy of confrontation could attach its full legal conviction to the Quadripartite Agreement. That would amount to making the Agreement a weapon designed to make the other side capitulate in Berlin.

Such action would clearly contradict the intentions of the Agreement's authors. The four governments have expressly stated that they "will strive to promote the elimination of tension and the prevention of complications in the relevant area." For this very purpose they have promised mutually to "respect their individual and joint rights and responsibilities which remain unchanged." This formula may seem ambiguous: The contents of those rights and responsibilities is controversial between East and West. The controversial nature, however, has been in the minds of the negotiators to the full; it was only after they had decided to drop the legal aspects as an utterly intractable topic that agreement had become possible.11/ In the wording of the Quadripartite Agreement, the consensus that has finally been reached has to be understood as being "irrespective of the differences in legal views." That means _inter_ _alia_ that the rights and responsibilities that require mutual respect also include the respective interpretations attached to them. Either side must accept that the other side tries to invoke its legal views--up to a limit where such advocacy would become tantamount to political attacks against "the situation developed in the area," i.e., against the status quo enjoyed by the contractual partner.

The political wisdom that the authors of the Quadripartite Agreement have adhered to recognizes that there are basic issues between East and West that cannot possibly be solved. Yet it is indispensable at the same

---

10. Cf. ibid., pp. 41-43.

11. Cf. ibid., pp. 94-96.

time to reduce tensions and to prevent crisis by mutual agreement in troubled areas. Such purpose can be accomplished only if one does not insist that the basic differences have to be overcome. The contracting parties must concentrate their efforts on procedures that will allow them to get along with one another in the future despite all remaining basic controversy.

The text of the Quadripartite Agreement recognizes such procedures: It does not define the rights and responsibilities of the contracting parties; nor is it specific on the nature of topics like "transit traffic" or "ties." Instead, it defines what each side will do when certain cases of transit traffic, West Berlin-West German ties, etc. are on the agenda of everyday life. The relevant question is not which political meaning and objective one side or the other should envisage, but rather which kind of procedure must be mutually observed so that open conflict (to be expected on grounds of past experience) can be avoided.

Accordingly, the Quadripartite Agreement provided inter alia for "transit traffic by road, rail and waterways" through East German territory, and specified that such traffic should "receive the most simple, expeditious and preferential treatment provided by international practice." A number of very detailed provisions made clear how these norms were to be translated into concrete practice. At the same time there was no word whatsoever on the problem whether the transit traffic was to be regarded as a correlate to Western right of original presence in Berlin and hence as an imposed obligation on the GDR (as the Western Powers think) or rather as a freely accepted contractual promise that was in full consonance with the idea of unlimited GDR sovereignty (as the Eastern viewpoint sees it). A similar relationship between precise practical arrangements and missing statements on matters of principle can be observed also with regard to the other topics of the Quadripartite Agreement. That can be termed the "logic of modus vivendi."

Developments in Berlin, 1972-1974

The Quadripartite Agreement went into effect on June 3, 1972. Despite opposing interpretations in matters of political principle, the contracting parties by and large have managed to contain their conflicts and to get along with one another on the basis of the procedures established by the treaty. There have been many opposing claims and mutual protests, but relatively few acute confrontations. This applies in particular to the handling of the traffic between West Berlin and West Germany, which is regarded as the cornerstone of Soviet trustworthiness by the Western governments.

However, the East-West interaction in Berlin has not been consistently smooth. There have been occasional controversies over the margin of discretion which may be claimed by the East German authorities. Both the USSR and the GDR take the view that unimpeded transit traffic is a freely accepted obligation that cannot possibly limit East German sovereignty. It follows from this argument that, in single cases, basic and urgent needs of the GDR may take precedence over the requirement of transit in the easiest and fullest possible manner. Such a perception clearly underlies much of what East German representatives have argued when they were confronted with West German complaints from time to time. Soviet spokesmen have occasionally shown their support for this kind of approach.12/

In mid-1974, the West German Bundestag decided to found a Federal Office for Environmental Protection in West Berlin after the three Western Powers had given their approval. Such a step ran directly counter to what the USSR had established as its interpretation of the Quadripartite Agreement. According to Moscow's theses (which had been loudly proclaimed before as a "warning" to the West), activities of federal agencies in West Berlin have to be regarded as generally illegal. The Soviet Union, however, had tolerated that situation thus far. Moscow had added that it would certainly not acquiesce in any enlargement of the presence of federal agencies in West Berlin. Soviet opposition, which was duly supported by the other Warsaw Pact countries, was aggravated by the fact that the creation of new federal agencies in West Berlin openly underscored the claim of the three Western Powers that they alone were entitled to decide West Berlin's status problems and that the USSR had no right to participate.

The Soviet Union and East Germany threatened punitive action in case the Bundestag ruling should be implemented. They officially declared that they would then be "forced to take corresponding measures," and indicated that the staff members of the Federal Office for Environmental Protection would not be permitted free transit.13/ On July 29, 1974, the GDR invoked this policy in a first case. This action caused great alarm in the Western capitals. More than anything else, the conflict at the access routes was seen as a matter of

---

12. Cf. ibid., pp. 161-162 and 178-183.

13. Ministries of Foreign Affairs of the German Democratic Republic and the Soviet Union, Das Vierseitige Abkommen ueber Westberlin und seine Realisierung. Dokumente 1971-1977 (Berlin [East]: Staatsverlag der DDR, 1977), pp. 187-190.

political principle with far-reaching practical implications: Could the GDR deny transit unilaterally at its free discretion? Would that not entail tacit Western agreement to any further transit restrictions that the GDR might choose to enact?

Therefore, Washington took strong counteraction. The United States administration made clear in Moscow that the bilateral trade agreement would be dropped if the situation at the transit routes did not normalize. East Germany got word that diplomatic relations could be started only if there were no acute conflict over Berlin. There was no further denial of transit. The USSR and the GDR, however, were given the satisfaction that the Western Powers tacitly agreed that no additional federal agency should be created in West Berlin.

The crisis-like situation in summer 1974 proved to be a short episode. However, it was to have far-reaching psychological consequences for years to come. Soviet suspicions had been aroused that the Federal Republic of Germany planned to use the Quadripartite Agreement for changes in West Berlin to its favor. Consequently, the latent East-West conflict over the nature and the extent of West Berlin's legitimate ties to West Germany intensified strongly.

Until summer 1974, both the USSR and the GDR had issued comparatively few official protests against ties between West Berlin and West Germany. They had, however, made clear that they regarded the city as a "separate political entity" and wanted the Western side to comply with that concept. In a number of cases the controversy was bridged by ambivalent compromise formulas. Nonetheless, some bitter conflicts had emerged. The Soviet Union, and consequently its allies, seized the political profit of a refusal to do business with the federal institutions located in West Berlin, asserting that they could not be expected to legitimize their existence. For this very reason the program which was to implement the Soviet-West German agreement on cultural cooperation remained unsigned during Brezhnev's Bonn visit in spring 1973 (and since then). Another controversy involved the Federal Republic's competence to care of West Berliners abroad as permitted by the three Western Powers and stated in the Quadripartite Agreement. In summer 1973, the USSR came to restrict that competence to natural persons only, thereby excluding juridical persons.

Critical Conflict Over Berlin, 1974-1978

The conflicts that had evolved until early 1974 intensified greatly and proliferated thereafter. For years to come there were only very few categories of ties that went unchallenged by the USSR and the GDR. Both Moscow and East Berlin regularly suspected that visits of official federal representatives in West Berlin were designed to demonstrate federal authority over the city, that West German laws and treaties being extended to West Berlin had the sole aim of making the city a federal "Land," that both official and societal West German assemblies taking place in West Berlin constituted something similar to a peaceful conquest, and so forth. Accordingly, there was a plethora of Soviet official protests, warnings, refusals to cooperate, and counteractions. The GDR, though not a party to the Quadripartite Agreement, claimed a similar right to watch over its "correct" implementation by West Berlin and West Germany.

The situation in Berlin repeatedly became rather tense. Eastern polemics against Western behavior in the city intensified. The federal institutions in West Berlin came under full Eastern boycott. An additional field of controversy arose when the USSR and the GDR began to oppose West Berlin's inclusion in the European Community, which had been tolerated consistently since the early 1950s. There were even several incidents at the access routes which could be conceivably interpreted as attempts to interfere with the domestic affairs of West Berlin. Frequent threats implied that unimpeded transit could be counted upon only in case of compliance with Eastern theses on the Quadripartite Agreement. Such Soviet and East German behavior ran counter to the obligation (laid down in the "General Provisions" of the Quadripartite Agreement) that the contracting parties refrain from the "use or threat of force in the area" and settle their disputes "solely by peaceful means."

Subsiding Conflict in Berlin Since 1978

Finally, however, reason prevailed. Brezhnev's visit in Bonn at the beginning of May 1978, marked the turning point (despite the fact that a few of the necessary adjustments took some additional months). Obviously, the West German representatives, particularly Chancellor Schmidt, managed to convince Brezhnev that they intended neither to increase their competences with regard to West Berlin nor to snub the USSR. The Soviet leaders were nonetheless interested in a cooperative relationship with Bonn for general policy reasons. The exchange of views seems to have resulted in a kind of standstill agreement. The West Germans were willing to take into account Soviet sensitivities more fully than previously. The Soviet politicians responded by more or less respecting Western interpretations of the Quadripartite Agreement: Whenever they would protest against them in the future, in order to protect their legal standpoint, they would be careful not to exert acute pressure and thus to incite tension.

Mutual restraint was to be the watchword of Berlin policies. The tacit agreement reached in May 1978 did not imply that either of the two sides gave up its basic interpretation of the legal situation in Berlin. The point was rather to improve relations by avoiding those steps that were perceived as particularly provocative by the other side.

Two cases illustrate well how the tacit agreement of May 1978 works in practice. In the fall of 1978, the Lord Mayor of West Berlin was due to take the chair in the Bonn "Laender" representation (the Bundesrat) according to West German legal procedures. Both the USSR and the GDR long had strongly warned against this action, arguing that this would make the Lord Mayor a federal government official and thus incorporate West Berlin into the Federal Republic. From the West German standpoint, however, the Eastern demand was tantamount to foreign interference into the domestic legal order and that could not be accepted. Therefore, the Lord Mayor of West Berlin finally took the chair in the Bundesrat. At the same time, however, Moscow was assured that the Lord Mayor in his Bundesrat function would scrupulously abstain from anything that would give him an official federal function. In particular, he would not act as deputy to the federal President and not sign federal laws on his behalf. The Soviet Union honored this West German restraint by restricting its reaction to verbal protests.

Another case in point is West Berlin's participation in the direct elections to the European Parliament in mid-1979. Despite the fact that the three Western Powers had provided for the West Berliners to take part in those elections only indirectly, the USSR and the GDR had persisted in their view that the EC Parliament was acquiring a new political quality and that the city was not entitled to be incorporated into such a state-like West European institution. On the other side, both Western and West German representatives argued that West Berlin's relationship to the EC was not to undergo any basic change whatsoever. When the elections finally took place, Moscow issued only angry protests and comments. In addition, it authorized the GDR to eliminate the special status of the East Berlin representatives in the East German Volkskammer.14/ With

---

14. "Rechtsordung unserer Republik wird wieder vervoll-kommnet," _Neues Deutschland_, June 29, 1979; Mai Pod-kliuchnikov, "Neopravdannaia shumikha," _Pravda_, July 2, 1979; and interview by Ambassador P. Abrassimov, _Neues Deutschland_, September 3, 1979.

this action, one of the few remaining symbols of East Berlin's special status was abandoned--an obvious step of symbolic retaliation that, however, did not amount to full negation of the special status (a semblance of which the three Western Powers regard as indispensable and as part of the status quo legally cemented by the Quadripartite Agreement).

Travel Regulations as a Problem

In 1970-1971, one of the basic Western demands had been that the West Berliners, who had been isolated from the surroundings of their city and from their relatives and friends living there, be given visiting rights in East Berlin and in the GDR. After some debate the USSR had made substantial concessions in the Quadripartite Agreement. When subsequently representatives of West Berlin and East Germany worked out the details, their agreement extended also to the sum of money to be exchanged into Eastern marks by the West Berliners. However, the West Berlin negotiators did not want to present themselves as accomplices of the deal in public, as the fixation of a compulsory exchange rate meant in fact that the West Berliners who visited relatives and friends in the East had to pay twice: for presents eagerly sought by their hosts and for the Western currency needs of the GDR State Bank.15/ Therefore, the compulsory exchange rate as agreed upon was not publicly included into the final agreement. The government of the GDR, however, formally acknowledged that the currency exchange rate was part of the understanding reached in the course of the negotiations.16/
Twice--in summer 1973 and 1979--there have been

---

15. The visitors from the West are expected by their East German hosts to bring with them highly appreciated Western goods and highly valued Western money. In return, the hosts usually provide food, accommodations, and also largely the costs for servies such as trains and busses. In addition, it is very difficult for Westerners to buy goods in the GDR. The choice is limited both in quantity and quality; the more attractive goods often may not be taken home across the frontier. Therefore, the sums of money to be exchanged are normally rather useless and represent a double burden.

16. Dokumentation zur Anordnung der Regierung der DDR ueber die Durchfuerung des verbindlichen Mindestumtauschs von Zahlungsmitteln vom 5. November 1973 (Berlin: Press and Information Office of the Land Berlin, January 1974), pp. 2-4.

East German attempts to arbitrarily restrict the influx
of West Berliners into the eastern part of the city
temporarily during large-scale youth meetings there.
Such measures, however, could not be justified on
grounds of the agreements reached in 1971. Western
protests caused the GDR to drop the planned restrictions.

The East German authorities, however, soon found a
more efficient instrument to restrict the contacts
between their citizens and the West Berliners. They
were quite aware that the compulsory exchange rate had
the function of an "entrance fee" for visiting Western
relatives and friends and also was generally regarded as
such. Consequently, they decided to raise that fee
whenever they wanted to increase the protection of the
population against Western contacts. They simply
exploited the fact that the compulsory exchange rate had
not been publicized as part of the East-West agreement.

In November 1973, the GDR unilaterally doubled the
compulsory exchange rate and cancelled most of the
exemptions that had been in force until then.17/ There
was a sharp decrease in the number of visitors during
the following year. The West German government made
strong efforts to induce the GDR to withdraw its
measures. In November 1974, the East German government
reduced the compulsory exchange rate by 35 percent; one
month later the exemptions that had been granted earlier
were restored. These concessions were compensated for
by economic counterconcessions of the Federal Republic.
Again the deal, though explicit, was not made public,
since the East German negotiators had argued that the
GDR was a sovereign state that could not openly admit
that its domestic affairs were subject to interstate
agreement. Therefore, the East German concessions took
the form of intrastate measures. At the same time,
however, the West German counterconcessions were
contractually formalized.18/

The limited public status of the mutual obligations
provided the political basis for the new restrictions
the GDR imposed in October 1980. The destabilizing
events in Poland created extreme anxiety in the East
German ruling circles. Seclusion against both the
neighbors in the East and in the West became the
dominant interest of the SED (Sozialistische Einheitspartei Deutschlands) leadership. Increasing the compulsory currency exchange rate was again the means of

---

17. Ibid., pp. 15-16.

18. Texte zur Deutschlandpolitik (Bonn: Federal Ministry
for Intra-German Relations, July 1976), vol. II/2, pp.
277-278, 339-340, 405-407.

restricting Western visits. The rate was doubled; all exemptions were cancelled.19/ The measures were designed to hit particularly older pensioners with sufficient time for travel and younger people with families who wanted to see relatives and friends beyond the Eastern border: The pensioners had to incur costs from which they had been spared so far, and young families had to pay several times as much when they brought their children with them. After the increases visits from West Berlin to the Eastern part of the city and to the GDR decreased by roughly 60 percent.

If one applies the mildest possible criteria, the GDR government has thus circumvented the travel arrangements contained in the Quadripartite Agreement and in the follow-up agreements. It has certainly acted contrary to the obligation as expressed in the Quadripartite Agreement "to facilitate visits and travel by permanent residents of the Western sectors of Berlin." It does not then, meet its contractual commitment of December 20, 1971, "to make a contribution to detente" and therefore "to facilitate and improve travel and visits by persons with permanent residence in Berlin (West)."

THE RELATIONSHIP BETWEEN THE USSR AND ITS
EAST EUROPEAN ALLIES

The policies of East Berlin are under rather tight Soviet control. The line to be followed is determined by Moscow; the allies, including the GDR as the most vitally concerned Warsaw Pact state, have to act within the framework set by the USSR. In the case of differences, East Germany may diverge only to an extent that does not harm Soviet interests.20/ Seen from Moscow, there is a stringent logic to this kind of relationship: As any serious conflict over Berlin involves the three Western Powers, particularly the United States, it is

---

19. _Neues Deutschland_, October 10, 1980. Cf. Federal Ministry for Intra-German Relations, _Informationen_ No. 19 (1980):13-16.

20. For historical cases and developments see Gerhard Wettig, "East Berlin under the Shadow of Soviet Policy," _The German Tribune_, June 26, 1969, pp. 7 and 16; Gerhard Wettig, "The Berlin Policy of the USSR and the GDR," _Aussenpolitik: German Foreign Affairs Review_ No. 2 (1970):144-149; and Gerhard Wettig, _Community and Conflict in the Socialist Camp: The Soviet Union, East Germany and the German Problem 1965-1972_ (New York: St. Martin's and London: Hurst, 1975), pp. 9-19, 82-117.

the USSR--not the GDR--that has to commit its resources. Therefore the nation that has taken the responsibility also must be in control of the events for which it will be held responsible.

The pattern repeatedly becomes transparent on minor occasions, particularly in matters of transit traffic. When the USSR strongly protested against President Carter's visit in West Berlin in Chancellor Schmidt's company on July 15, 1978, the authorities of the GDR seem to have sensed Soviet support for delaying measures at the access routes. This aroused most vigorous Western protests to the relevant Soviet agencies--which, in turn, denied any Eastern intention to hinder the transit traffic. The Soviet statements were quite serious--and the GDR government that was being strongly reproached by Bonn saw fit to explain the events by a misunderstanding on the part of subordinate authorities and not to repeat the traffic aggravations on similar future occasions.21/

The West Berlin policy dictated by Moscow as a rule is faithfully followed by the other Warsaw Pact states, even if they see no interest of their own and it complicates their relations with the Federal Republic. A telling example has been provided by Poland since summer 1973. When Warsaw had accepted diplomatic relations with Bonn in December 1970, it had easily consented to the protection both of natural and juridical persons from West Berlin by the West German representation. In summer 1973, however, Moscow made the question of juridical persons a point of sharp controversy. Czechoslovakia, and later Hungary, were caused to make diplomatic relations with West Germany conditional upon Bonn's acceptance of juridical persons from West Berlin not being represented.22/ The Polish government adapted

---

21. "Protest der Westmaechte gegen 'Nadelstiche' im Transitverkehr," Frankfurter Allgemeine Zeitung, July 17, 1978; "Westmaechte protestieren gegen Behinderungen auf den Transitwegen," Der Tagesspiegel, July 18, 1978; and "Westalliierte Protestnote an Ostberliner Sowjetbotschaft," Sueddeutsche Zeitung, July 20, 1978.

22. This was in contradiction to an informal agreement reached during the quadripartite negotiations; see information passed to the Foreign Relations Committee of the Bundestag by Ministerial Director van Well (Foreign Ministry), as quoted in full in "Protokoll stuetzt Bonner Position gegenueber Moskau," Die Welt, October 3, 1973. Cf. Hartmut Schiedermair, Der voelkerrechtliche Status Berlins nach dem Viermaechte-Abkommen (Berlin: Springer Verlag, 1975), pp. 173-186; and Honore M. Catadul, Jr. A Balance Sheet of the Quadripartite Agreement

itself to the new situation by editing an intrastate decree to the effect that legal affairs with West Berlin--in contrast to those with West Germany (which continued to pass through the diplomatic representation of the Federal Republic)--had to be handled by the Polish Military Mission in West Berlin.23/

The degree to which Moscow is setting the path for the smaller Warsaw Pact states is visible also from the text of the relevant mutual assistance treaties. On October 7, 1975, the USSR concluded a bilateral assistance treaty with the GDR. It contained a clause obliging the contracting parties to "maintain and develop their connections with West Berlin taking into account that it is no part of the Federal Republic of Germany and cannot be governed by it."24/ The formula had been taken from the Quadripartite Agreement, but modified so as to fit the Soviet interpretation: The term "connections" ("Verbindungen") replaced, following an option provided as a possibility by the Russian equivalent ("sviazi"), "ties"; the same applies to the wording "part" (going back to the Russian "sostavnaia chast'") instead of "constituent part." Thus the Soviet postulate that West Berlin is a state-like entity to be kept totally separate from the Federal Republic, was to be confirmed. At the same time, the special relationship ("ties") which according to the Quadripartite Agreement existed between West Berlin and West Germany, was applied to the city's relations with the two Eastern states.

In 1977, the smaller Warsaw Pact states, with the notable exception of Rumania, concluded similar mutual assistance treaties with the GDR. In all the cases, the paragraph on the relationship with West Berlin contained exactly the same wording as the Soviet-East German treaty of 1975.25/ In Rumania's case, there was only a bilateral declaration of friendship and cooperation, the text of which was less rigid. The authors of the declaration demanded "renunciation of any attempt to violate the special status of West Berlin" and confirmed their "resolution to maintain and develop manifold

---

(Berlin: Berlin Verlag, 1978), pp. 112-113.

23. Cf. Schiedermair, _Der voelkerrechtliche Status Berlins_, pp. 160-161.

24. _Pravda_, October 8, 1975 and _Neues Deutschland_, October 8, 1975.

25. See _Neues Deutschland_, March 26-27, 1977 (Hungary); May 31, 1977 (Poland); September 14, 1977 (Bulgaria); and October 4, 1977 (Czechoslovakia).

relations to West Berlin."26/ It is safe to assume that Bucharest's verbal restraint was due to its interest in demonstrating independence to the West Germans (which was expected to pay off economically). As early as in 1976, however, the USSR had made Rumania follow the general Eastern line in boycotting the federal institutions located in West Berlin.27/

BERLIN IN THE GLOBAL EAST-WEST RELATIONSHIP

The Soviet leadership clearly seeks to keep Europe quiet so as to prevent situations that might ignite open political conflict between the two superpowers and their alliances--a conflict that could escalate and thus threaten the USSR with incalculable risk and damage. Such Soviet interest, however, does not mean that Moscow is willing to acquiesce in anything that, in Soviet perception, could result in a deterioration of the status quo, as the contest about the establishment of the Federal Environmental Office in West Berlin plainly indicated. Accordingly, there has been extreme Soviet sensitivity in this respect. After the Brezhnev-Schmidt understanding of May 1978, much of the formerly expressed Soviet suspicion has subsided and given way to policies of mutual restraint--but there is still a potential of suspicion left that could be reactivated.
In the course of the missile deployment controversy from 1979 to 1983, both the USSR and the GDR have occasionally sought to impress the West Germans with the prospect of danger to West Berlin. However, when NATO finally began to deploy the missiles and the Federal Republic did not yield to Soviet pressure on the issue, the threatened "ice age" from the East failed to materialize. Indeed, both the Soviet Union and East Germany initially hastened to increase cooperation with Bonn for a number of political and economic reasons. It was only in the wake of renewed Soviet-U.S. diplomatic activity later in 1984 that this line was finally abandoned.28/ Occasionally the Soviets sought to shift the status quo in Berlin slightly in its favor, serving

----

26. Neues Deutschland, June 11-12, 1977.

27. See the text of the Bucharest Warsaw Pact Declaration of November 26, 1976: Pravda, November 27, 1976 or Neues Deutschland, November 27, 1976.

28. See my detailed analysis in "The Present Soviet View on Trends in Germany," forthcoming in the Rand PR-volume on the October 1984 conference in Ebenhausen.

to remind the West of Berlin's latent instability.29/

At the same time, the Berlin problem serves a global political function for the USSR. There are various weak points and danger spots in the political posture of the Soviet Union. The east-central European scene is potentially unstable, as the case of Poland clearly shows and the anxious seclusion policies of the GDR indicate. Both countries, however, depend on Western economic cooperation and even on Western economic assistance for their (relative) material well-being, which is also a very important factor of domestic stability. The resulting requirement of cooperativeness with the West is strongly counteracted by seclusionist policies (designed to protect the Eastern population from allegedly "subversive" contact with Western people), particularly if those policies run counter to existing contractual commitments (as is the case with the GDR). Economic retaliation by Western countries, in particular the Federal Republic, is a priori not wholly implausible. The vulnerable situation of West Berlin, however, can serve the USSR and its allies as a reminder to the West that such retaliation can provoke counter-retaliation. Moscow has repeatedly hinted that the Berlin situation can be expected to remain quiet as long as the West sticks to the overall context of detente.30/

This also applies to wider aspects of Soviet policies toward the West. Since the mid-1970s, the Soviet leadership is increasingly dissatisfied with the political line taken by the United States. The post-Afghanistan developments (which, in Soviet presentation, are due to reasons other than Soviet military action in the central Asian country) are seen as but a temporary climax of allegedly principled "anti-Soviet" sentiment. Seen from Moscow, there is acute danger that the "anti-detente" forces in Washington cause a sharp political and military shift against the USSR in all of NATO and steer a course of global East-West confrontation. Such an effect is clearly feared by the Soviet leadership. For this purpose, the Soviet Union tries to bring to bear those interests in the West which make a continuation of detente policies in Europe imperative. The common interest of the Federal Republic and the Western Powers to safeguard West Berlin, is ranks foremost in this political strategy.

Accordingly, it cannot be regarded as an indication

---

29. Cf., e.g., "A Soviet Shoot-Down Threat," Washington Post, April 22, 1985.

30. Cf. Soviet press declaration of May 22, 1976 in Pravda, May 22, 1976.

of European "decoupling" from world politics when, in the period after the Afghanistan intervention, Eastern peacefulness and even cooperativeness on the European theater sharply contrasted to intensive East-West tensions elsewhere. It was a deliberate Soviet choice to employ detente and restraint in Europe, particularly in Berlin, as a counterinstrument against developments in other parts of the world which were viewed apprehensively in Moscow. The fact that Europe and Berlin cannot hope to prosper peacefully when global conditions are not favorable became more clearly visible after the Polish turmoil in the early 1980s. Those West Berliners who profited from the East-West agreements through freer travels and visits were the first to pay for the deterioration of the East-West climate which was beginning to take place. If violent action had been taken in Poland, as it has been taken in Afghanistan, the Berlin situation would inevitably have been most gravely affected.

7

Berlin and East German-Soviet Relations

Edwina Moreton

Ever since the creation of two separate German states in 1949, the German Democratic Republic (GDR) has claimed "Berlin"--that is, all of Berlin--as its capital. Over 30 years later, the continued existence of West Berlin as a walled-in enclave on East German territory challenges East Germany's claim to full sovereignty under international law. But East Germany's chances of resolving the Berlin problem to its own satisfaction are slim, not just because of the continued presence of the three Western Powers and Western troops in the city, but also because Berlin as a whole remains to this day under Four-power status and because the fourth Power, the Soviet Union, has a vested interest in keeping it that way.

East Germany is the Soviet Union's closest ally in Eastern Europe. Yet their close political relationship has not prevented recurrent disagreements over Berlin. But however strongly it feels on the subject, East Germany, of all the states in Eastern Europe, is the one most restricted in its ability to pursue its own national interests. Special legal, military, economic and political factors condition Soviet-East German relations and limit East Germany's room for maneuver in the German problem.

The German Democratic Republic was granted sovereignty by the Soviet Union in 1955, shortly after West Germany acquired its sovereignty from the Western Allies. According to the various declarations and notes exchanged at the time, East Germany was free to decide its own internal and foreign policy, including its relations with West Germany.1/ However, the Soviet Union

---

1. These include the Soviet declaration of March 25, 1954; the treaty with the Soviet Union of September 20, 1955; and the exchange of notes which accompanied the treaty.

retained those functions deriving from the agreements between the four Powers concerning the maintenance of security. Significantly, the nature and direction of these Powers was not specified. The Soviet Union further "took note" of East German declarations concerning its observance of the principles of the Potsdam Agreement of 1945. The interpretation of this point is important. East Germany was later to anchor its claim to full and unimpeded sovereignty to the fact that, since it had fulfilled all the stipulations of the Potsdam Agreement with respect to denazification, demilitarization, etc., it was therefore absolved of any further Four-power jurisdiction. The Soviet Union has never flatly contradicted the East German claim. Nor has it ever formally accepted the claim. The Soviet Union has consistently maintained its residual responsibility for the whole of Germany ("ganz Deutschland"), which it derives from the Four-power agreements. Much to East Germany's irritation, this point was confirmed in the 1964 friendship treaty between the GDR and the Soviet Union and also in the Four-power Berlin Agreement of 1971.

MILITARY CONSTRAINTS

The restrictions on East German sovereignty are most clearly expressed in its military relationships with its Soviet protector. The Soviet Union continues to maintain 19 full-strength divisions in East Germany, far more than in any other Warsaw Pact state. Although East Germany forms the front line in any armed conflict between East and West in Europe, the task of the Soviet divisions is not simply to defend the GDR's western borders. They also embody the Soviet Union's continuing rights in Germany as one of the four Powers, and in East Germany as an occupation power.

The presence of Soviet troops on the territory of its Warsaw Pact allies is in each case governed by special treaty. According to the treaty governing the allegedly "temporary" stationing of Soviet troops in East Germany, signed in 1957, the Soviet Union can move its troops, conduct maneuvers on East German territory and even declare a state of emergency in East Germany without reference to the East German government. These special provisions of the East German-Soviet troop treaty are more than symbolic and remain in force to this day.

The same is true of East Germany's special status within the Warsaw Pact. The GDR's full participation in the Pact was delayed to await the final outcome of Soviet initiatives on German reunification. At least theoretically the possibility was left open for the withdrawal of the GDR from the Pact into a united Germany, within an all-European security system. Even the wording of the Warsaw treaty discriminates against the GDR, which in the event of attack on any member state was unable to decide for itself what assistance to give--this was to be decided by its allies.2/ Furthermore, the East German armed forces (Nationale Volksarmee, NVA) remain the only national armed forces in Eastern Europe wholly and directly subordinate to Warsaw Pact, i.e., Soviet, command.

ECONOMIC FACTORS

The particular economic constraints on East Germany are less obvious. The East German economy has proved to be one of the driving forces behind the integration of the Council for Mutual Economic Assistance (CMEA). Because of its lack of many important raw materials (especially gas and oil, but also iron ore, cotton, etc.), the GDR is heavily dependent on its partners in the CMEA. Its economy is especially suited to benefit from economic specialization and the international division of labor within the CMEA. Despite the relative ease with which the GDR has built up a hard currency trade with West Germany (through preferential credits and the loophole in EEC regulations which allows East German products to be classed as "German" and therefore exempt from normal tariffs), the East German economy will remain very closely bound to the CMEA and to trade with the Soviet Union in particular.

POLITICAL CONTROLS

But it is the political constraints which bind East Germany most closely into Soviet foreign policy on the national question. The Soviet Union remains East Germany's protecting power. And until the general recognition of the GDR in the 1970s, the Soviet Union was East Germany's only influential channel to the outside world. The Soviet Union is involved in the German problem on several different levels. It is not only East Germany's major ally, it is also one of the four Powers with residual responsibilities for Germany as a whole. As such it has a vested interest in European affairs in general and in west European affairs in particular. At the same time it is a superpower with global interests,

---

2. Boris Meissner, "The Soviet Union's Bilateral Pact System in Eastern Europe," in Eastern Europe in Transition, ed. Kurt London (Baltimore: Johns Hopkins Press, 1966).

commitments and security concerns. At times these different aspects of Soviet foreign policy come into conflict with each other. For East Germany the main priority for most of the postwar period has been the resolution of its national question and the fight for diplomatic recognition. For the Soviet Union, East Germany's interests have not always taken precedence. East Germany remains caught in this web of Soviet foreign policy interests, as the examples of the two most recent Berlin "crises" have shown.

During the crisis which led to the construction of the Berlin wall, in August 1961, the divergence in Soviet and East German objectives was particularly marked. In 1958 Khrushchev threatened to abrogate uni- laterally the provisions of Potsdam and "normalize" the situation in Berlin--meaning ultimately denying any legal basis for Western presence in or access to Berlin, turning West Berlin into a demilitarized free city, and leaving the Western Powers to negotiate all access to the city with the "sovereign" East German government. East Germany stuck to its claim of sovereignty over "Berlin", but as the crisis progressed it became clear that the Soviet objective was really something dif- ferent. By allowing several supposed deadlines for action to lapse and by opting in the end for the con- struction of the wall, leaving Western access rights untouched, the Soviet Union made it clear that what it really wanted was a confirmation of the status quo and an end to the destabilization of the GDR by stopping the flow of refugees across the border inside Berlin.

The wall was very much a minimum objective for the GDR regime--if a vitally important one. Throughout the campaign, Walter Ulbricht, the East German leader, in- sisted that the whole of Berlin was the present capital of the GDR and the future capital of all Germany. The increasingly divergent statements on the crisis repre- sented far more than a division of labor between East Germany and the Soviet Union. By again insisting that the GDR was absolved from the conditions of the Potsdam Agreement, Ulbricht was implicitly attacking the Soviet position as one of the four Powers. The decision by the Soviet Union not to interfere with Western access to the city was seen by East Germany as representing an unwil- ling East German concession of an existing right.3/

The negotiation of the 1971 Quadripartite Agreement on Berlin produced another crisis, but this time exclu- sively in East German-Soviet relations. By blocking a

---

3. The divergence between the East German and Soviet Positions is explored more fully in Edwina Moreton, East Germany and the Warsaw Alliance: The Politics of Detente (Boulder: Westview Press, 1978), pp. 25-28.

settlement over Berlin in 1970-71 which fell short of his maximum objectives, Ulbricht was proving a major obstacle to progress in West Germany's Ostpolitik and the Soviet Union's Westpolitik.

Although the Soviet Union would not have countenanced any direct challenge to the stability of the GDR, after nearly thirty years West Germany had made the important concession that two separate German states existed. This opened the way for the widespread international recognition of the GDR. However West Germany continued to insist that relations between the two states were of a special nature; it was not prepared to accord the GDR full international recognition, since it upheld the goal of German reunification. The Soviet Union was prepared to lend verbal support to East Germany in its continuing argument with West Germany, but was not prepared to make full diplomatic recognition by West Germany a precondition for all further progress in the Ostpolitik.

The argument over Berlin produced a crisis of confidence in East German-Soviet relations which was only resolved by the removal from power of Ulbricht in May 1971 and his replacement by Erich Honecker.4/ The Four-power Berlin Agreement was signed a few months later. However, East German claims to sovereignty over Berlin were not dropped. The style of East German policy has changed under Erich Honecker, but its long-term objective remains the same. Both the Soviet Union and East Germany have sought to interpret the 1971 Berlin Agreement as restrictively as possible--particularly with respect to the ties permitted between West Germany and West Berlin. However, the Soviet Union still retains its undefined "residual rights" for both Berlin and for Germany as a whole, while the GDR insists on its unrestricted sovereignty over "Berlin."5/

Despite its otherwise full acceptance into the international community, East Germany still finds itself constrained by the unresolved national question. The continued Four-power status of Berlin keeps the national question open in one area where it implies a dimunition of the East German case. On the one hand, West Germany has always been happy to rely on Four-power control to guarantee the continued existence of West Berlin. East Germany, on the other hand, claims no longer to be subject to Four-power control. Hence Soviet adherence

---

4. The Berlin issue was not the only issue at stake in the transfer of power. Nor was it the result of simple Soviet fiat. However, the Soviet Union has happy to lend its blessing to the change of leadership in the SED. Ibid., pp. 182-190.

5. Ibid., p. 220.

to the Four-power framework challenges East Germany's claim to Berlin as its capital. West Germany can live with these consequences of the unresolved national question. East Germany has to.

East Germany has been free to argue for its interpretation of the Quadripartite Berlin Agreement in its relations with third states. And particularly in the developing world the GDR has had some successes in encouraging states to refuse trade agreements and co-operation agreements with West Germany that also include West Berlin. Some Soviet-West German agreements have been held up for the same reason.

However, East Germany is still caught up in the wider net of Soviet policy on the German question. Because of West German interest in promoting increased contacts between the two German states in the name of national unity, the GDR is uniquely placed to help further Soviet foreign policy objectives in Western Europe. Particularly in view of the deteriorating relationship with the United States since the invasion of Afghanistan, the Soviet Union has usually had a clear interest in keeping channels open to West Germany. Any concession to West Germany in return for a closer relationship with the Soviet Union would almost always have to be at East Germany's expense. Thus, the potential for friction in East German-Soviet relations remains. Although Berlin is no longer the pulse of East-West relations and has clearly benefited from the decade of the East-West detente, it remains a thorny issue in East German-Soviet relations. Since the 1971 Berlin Agreement, the Soviet Union has tended to view improvements in the situation surrounding Berlin as a carrot to safeguard its improved relations with West Germany. However for East Germany, causing problems over Berlin is about the only stick it has left to wield in defense of its interpretation of the national question.

8

Berlin and the GDR: From Crisis Point to Bargaining Chip

Michael J. Sodaro

For the leaders of the German Democratic Republic (GDR), the twentieth anniversary of the construction of the Berlin wall was an occasion of grand festivity. Parades and speech-making heralded the event in East Berlin, where Erich Honecker, the First Secretary of the Socialist Unity party of Germany (SED) memorialized August 13, 1961 as a landmark in European history. Addressing a throng of over one hundred thousand East Berliners on holiday, Honecker lauded the actions of that day for having guaranteed "reliable control" and for countering "imperialist subversive activity" in the GDR.[1]/ Several weeks later, the tenor of official East German commentary marking the tenth anniversary of the signing of the Quadripartite Agreement on Berlin was considerably more subdued. Neues Deutschland, the SED's daily newspaper, unceremoniously recorded the date in an editorial appearing on page two.[2]/ Bureaucratically sober in tone, the commentary balanced modest praise for the agreement ("one of the important preconditions for the detente process in Europe") with warnings against the alleged violation of its provisions by the governments of the Federal Republic and West Berlin.

The starkly contrasting accents which the East German regime placed on the two anniversaries reflect important differences in the way the SED may perceive these commemorated events. From the regime's point of view, the construction of the Berlin wall in 1961, in spite of the worldwide propaganda backlash it provoked, was on the whole a positive achievement. It was the wall which put a virtual halt to the mass exodus of GDR citizens to the West, and thereby ended a process that threatened to undermine the very existence of the East

---

1. Neues Deutschland, August 14, 1981, pp. 1-2.

2. Ibid., September 3, 1981, p. 2.

109

German state. The SED's determination to celebrate the anniversary of the wall with public accolades to its effectiveness is a vivid indication that, far from recoiling at the fact of the wall, the East German leadership wishes to impress upon the population of the GDR (and, no doubt, upon the population and leadership of West Germany as well) the absolute necessity of maintaining the barrier as long as the internal security of the East German regime is at stake.

By contrast, the Quadripartite Agreement signed ten years later represented a setback to East German political interests, at least as they were defined by Honecker's predecessor at the helm of the SED, Walter Ulbricht. In effect, the Four-power accord imposed severe restrictions on the GDR's ability to interfere with Western traffic on the access routes between West Berlin and the Federal Republic, thus reducing the value of Berlin's disruptive potential to the East German leadership. Ulbricht himself was, in a sense, the principal "loser" of the Four-power agreement; in May 1971 he was removed from his position as head of the SED, in part because of Soviet impatience with his efforts to block not only the impending Berlin settlement, but the very process of Soviet and East European rapprochement with West Germany.

Given the importance which Berlin has acquired for the GDR over the years, how has the SED regime dealt with the problems surrounding the city since the end of World War II? What have been the chief opportunities for political and economic gains for the GDR arising from the Berlin situation, and what have been the principal vulnerabilities for the GDR stemming from Berlin? In addressing these questions, this brief essay makes no effort to be exhaustive. Rather it aims at assessing the pluses and minuses of the _Berlin-problematik_ over the past ten to twenty years as they might appear to the current rulers of the GDR. With this in mind, the approach taken here involves a quick survey of the chief functions Berlin has fulfilled for the GDR since the end of the war. Along the way, we shall pay special attention to the way these functions have affected not only the GDR's relationship with the West, but with the Soviet Union as well. Indeed, East German and Soviet interests in Berlin have not always been identical, and their policies have on more than one occasion diverged, at times sharply. The final section of the chapter attempts to draw up a balance sheet of the positive and negative features of the GDR's relationship with Berlin, focusing specifically on the period since the conclusion of the Four-power accord of 1971.

THE ULBRICHT ERA

Berlin has traditionally fulfilled three main political functions for the GDR. First, it has provided the East German leadership with the opportunity to extend the legal authority of the GDR, thereby enhancing its status and competence as a national actor in international affairs. Second, Berlin has played the role of a source of conflict by providing the GDR with the means to foment tensions in its relations with Bonn, often with the primary intention of blocking progress in inter-German relations or of reasserting the fundamental incompatibility of interests between the two German states in specific issues. Third, Berlin has functioned as a bargaining chip, enabling the GDR to pressure the West German government (or the West Berlin Senate) into making concessions of one kind or another in return for favorable actions by East Germany. In addition to these three political functions, Berlin has at various times also played an important economic role for the GDR, especially in recent years.

In all of these areas, the GDR has normally aligned its policies very carefully with Soviet positions on Berlin, usually following Moscow's lead on these matters or at least enlisting Soviet approval before undertaking initiatives of its own. There have been occasions, however, when Soviet wishes and East German actions have noticeably clashed. This was particularly the case during Ulbricht's tenure as chief of the SED.

Initially, the leaders of communist East Germany were careful not to stray very far from Soviet priorities in matters relating to Berlin. Even though Soviet policy with respect to Germany as a whole was rather tentative in the first several years following the conclusion of the war, the communists grouped around Walter Ulbricht tended for the most part to bend with the zigs and zags of Soviet policy. From the very outset of this early postwar period, Berlin occupied a position of major importance in this evolving Soviet-East German approach. Both the Soviets and the remnants of the Communist party of Germany (KPD) hoped to entice members of the Social Democratic party (SPD) into a working relationship with the communists, and Berlin, with its large SPD and KPD followings during the pre-Hitler era, was viewed as a convenient place to begin this process of collaboration. At first, the Soviet occupation authorities abjured a direct fusion of the two parties, but eventually shifted ground on this question. It was in Berlin that the issue of fusing the KPD and the SPD was most dramatically played out. Although the overwhelming majority of Berlin SPD voters who turned out for a special party referendum in March 1946 rejected outright fusion, it was an important segment of the Berlin SPD organization under Otto Grotewohl that ultimately opted to join with the communists in forming the SED in the following month.3/

As cold war tensions mounted during the next few years, East German policy tended to take a back seat to Soviet initiatives. Ulbricht provided full public support for the Berlin blockade of 1948-49 and for Moscow's interpretations of the legal status of Berlin. Needless to say, the SED was all too eager to support Soviet measures leading to the establishment of the German Democratic Republic in October 1949, although it is at least questionable whether the East German leadership under the feisty Ulbricht was content with the limited sovereignty accorded the new state by the Kremlin authorities.4/

Differences between the Soviet Union and the fledgling East German state first took a serious turn in 1953, and Berlin was the scene of the resulting conflict. According to the testimony of a former official in the East Berlin section of the SED, it was the Soviets who set in motion the events that led to the workers' uprising of June 17. Heinz Brandt, whose position in the party apparatus gave him access to inside information, subsequently disclosed that the spontaneous demonstrations by factory workers in East Berlin were in effect triggered by Lavrenti Beria's efforts to steal a march on his rivals in the Kremlin power struggle following Stalin's death.5/ In hopes of establishing a more relaxed atmosphere in Germany so as to pave the way for negotiations with the West aimed at settling the German problem, Beria pressured the SED into easing up on its economic austerity policies. Although Ulbricht gave in to most of these pressures, he balked at rescinding newly imposed work norms, and his hesitation on this issue brought the workers out into the streets. It took a massive display of Soviet power to quell the revolt. Once Beria's rivals regained control of the situation, they reinforced the USSR's commitment to maintaining the existence of the GDR and to supporting Ulbricht's personal exercise of power. The episode, however, had provided graphic evidence of the SED regime's double vulnerability. Not only did the regime lack popular support, but also the proximity of the West, particularly within the confines of Greater

---

3. On this period, see Henry Krisch, _German Politics under Soviet Occupation_ (New York: Columbia University Press, 1974).

4. The Soviets did not accord the GDR full legal sovereignty until 1957.

5. Heinz Brandt, _The Search for a Third Way_ (New York: Doubleday, 1970), pp. 184-220.

Berlin, left it exposed to even more potential disturbances than those faced by the GDR's East European neighbors.

The gravity of the Berlin problem became increasingly apparent over the course of the next eight years, as a rising number of East Germans took advantage of the open sectoral boundaries within the city to cross over into life in the West. It was in part because of this growing exodus that Nikita Khrushchev launched a protracted crisis over Berlin with his announcement in November 1958 that, unless the West agreed to Soviet terms, the USSR would denounce the Potsdam Agreement and grant the GDR the right to control traffic between the FRG and Berlin. (Foreign Minister Gromyko followed up this demarche by informing the three Western Powers that the Potsdam accord was no longer valid, and that West Berlin must be accorded the status of a "free city" within six months.) Although the Soviets unquestionably were concerned about the progressive disappearance of East Germany's population, it appears that Ulbricht and his East German colleagues nevertheless felt it necessary to maintain relentless pressure on the Kremlin to do something about the problem. Significantly, it was the GDR which first signaled the Soviet bloc's intention to press the West on Berlin when <u>Neues Deutschland</u> declared that "all Berlin lies on the territory of the GDR" in October 1958. Subsequently, Ulbricht engaged in strenuous efforts to persuade Khrushchev to make good on his pledge to sign a separate peace treaty with the GDR within six months. The Soviet leader was reluctant to take this step, however, and repeatedly pushed back the date of the threatened showdown with the West. By the spring 1960, Khrushchev was still counseling his nervous East German allies to be patient. Again in March 1961, Ulbricht returned empty-handed from a trip to Moscow during which he vigorously urged the Kremlin to take action. As late as July, with defections from the GDR running at nearly 1,000 a day, Khrushchev continued to resist the GDR's pleas for the conclusion of a separate peace treaty and for special measures to stem the flow of people leaving East Berlin.

By this time, the GDR had already put the West on notice that starting August 1, new regulations would take effect requiring Western planes in the designated air corridors to register with East Berlin traffic controllers. This move may have been undertaken by Ulbricht on his own since the Soviets showed no public inclination to enforce the new rules with their own air force. Finally, at a crucial session of the Warsaw Pact held in Moscow in early August Ulbricht was reportedly told that approval of his plan to close off West Berlin would be forthcoming only if the GDR could convincingly demonstrate that its security forces were capable of such an undertaking and that the GDR could withstand a cut-off of economic assistance from the West. After Ulbricht feverishly huddled with his associates in East Berlin, he returned to Moscow on August 5 with affirmative replies to both of these conditions. Shortly afterwards the Soviets agreed to proceed with the construction of the barriers separating the two parts of the city.6/

The construction of the wall provided a decisive response to the GDR's principal vulnerability with respect to Berlin up to that time, namely, its convenience as an escape route for GDR citizens. Berlin continued to pose problems of a serious nature in subsequent years, however, above all by serving as a communications outpost capable of beaming radio and television broadcasts to a large portion of GDR territory. Nevertheless, the wall itself placed the East German regime in a considerably more secure position than in the past, enabling it to take advantage of the opportunities offered by the Berlin situation. It was at this point that the GDR began to make greater use of the three political functions of the city noted above. In the process, Ulbricht and the SED increasingly collided with prevailing Soviet interests.

Three crises surrounding Berlin in the 1960s illustrate the GDR's position. In the spring of 1965, the West German government scheduled a plenary session of the Bundestag in West Berlin. The announcement of these plans triggered a vocal response from the Soviet Union as well as the GDR, both of whom rejected Bonn's contention that Berlin constituted an integral part of the Federal Republic. Although the Soviets were as committed to this view as their East German allies, they reportedly did not go as far as the GDR leadership had wished when it came to harassing the ground and air carriers that brought the Bundestag members to Berlin. Clearly, the Soviets were not interested in provoking a major crisis with the West over this issue. More significantly, the GDR exploited the tensions surrounding the incident by seeking to expand its legal competence regarding Berlin. In June 1965, the Foreign Minister of the GDR declared East German sovereignty over the air corridors leading to West Berlin from the Federal Republic. This assertion contradicted the rights not only of

---

6. Studies of the 1961 crisis include Robert M. Slusser, The Berlin Crisis of 1961 (Baltimore: Johns Hopkins University Press, 1973); Jack M. Schick, The Berlin Crisis, 1958-1962 (Philadelphia: University of Pennsylvania Press, 1971); Anita Dasbach-Mallinckrodt, Propaganda hinter der Mauer (Stuttgart: Kohlhammer, 1971); and Curtis Cate, The Ides of August (New York: M. Evans & Co., 1978).

the Western occupation authorities, but also of the USSR as well. The Soviets consequently cast a cold eye on the GDR's new claim, and the SED regime dropped further references to it until 1968. However, East German officials continued to insist that West Berlin was a part of the GDR (a view nominally supported by the Soviet Union), and went even further than recent Soviet statements by reaffirming that West Berlin must be demilitarized, a position from which the Soviets themselves had by this time retreated.7/

The next opportunity for East German action on Berlin occurred in the spring of 1968. In this critical period, the SED was deeply alarmed at the process of democratization taking place in Czechoslovakia and made no secret of its fears of West Germany's alleged efforts to turn the situation in Prague to its own advantage. Although Bonn treated the Czech reform movement with circumspection, it was a well-advertized aim of the grand coalition's Ostpolitik to normalize relations with the East European members of the Warsaw Pact, with a view to securing their acceptance of the FRG's positions on Berlin and other matters of vital interest to the GDR. It was in this context that the GDR took action to block the transit of West German government officials and party leaders between West Berlin and the Federal Republic in March and April, action that culminated in the GDR's refusal to allow West Berlin Mayor Klaus Schuetz to leave the city by car for the purpose of participating in a meeting of the Bundesrat in Bonn. On June 11, the GDR's Volkskammer went even further and established new passport and visa requirements for all West German travelers in the GDR, including those en route to and from West Berlin. In addition, minimum currency exchange rates were raised, new taxes on goods transported across GDR roads and waterways were introduced, and controls on printed matter allowed to pass through East German territory were stiffened.

Initially, the Soviets lent quick support to the GDR's actions, including those taken against Mayor Schuetz. However, the Kremlin displayed little enthusiasm in its expressions of solidarity with the SED. Indeed, it was reported that Ulbricht had been pressing the Kremlin for permission to introduce the passport and visa restrictions for several years, but without success.8/ Moscow's willingness to allow Ulbricht to go ahead with the scheme in June 1968 can best be explained

---

7. On the 1965 Berlin crisis, see Gerhard Wettig, _Conflict and Community in the Socialist Camp_ (London: C. Hurst, 1975), pp. 9-19.

8. _Der Spiegel_, June 17, 1968, p. 17.

with reference to Soviet apprehension over events in Czechoslovakia. But the Soviets made it plain that they were not interested in exacerbating matters. There was to be no tampering with Four-power transit privileges, a fact that Ulbricht publicly confirmed. Moreover, the Kremlin refrained from echoing Ulbricht's repeated assertions that West Berlin lay "on the territory of the GDR." Finally, in what could only be regarded as a personal affront to Ulbricht, the Soviet ambassador in the GDR, Abrassimov, met with Willy Brandt in Berlin and assured him of Moscow's lack of interest in any renewed outbreak of hostilities over the divided city.9/

The third incident took place in the first months of 1969. By this time the Soviet Union was manifestly interested in improving relations with West Germany, and recognized that only a relaxed international atmosphere would be conducive to an SPD victory in the federal elections set for October, an outcome which the Soviets plainly desired. Accordingly, when the grand coalition government announced that the Bundestag and the Bundesrat would convene in West Berlin to elect a new president, the Soviets opposed the move but consistently sought a negotiated compromise. On January 31, Abrassimov suggested in a hastily arranged conversation with Mayor Schuetz that the Soviets might be willing to arrange a new visitors' pass agreement permitting West Berliners to spend the coming Easter holidays with relatives living in East Berlin.10/ It was understood that in return the Soviets and the GDR expected the West German government to relocate the planned presidential election. Although West German authorities stated their preference for a broader visitors' pass (Passierschein)

---

9. The GDR must also have been irritated at the fact that Brandt came to Berlin in his role as West German Foreign Minister, and did not show his passport. Although the meeting was supposed to have been kept secret, the GDR reported it in Neues Deutschland. In the report, both Brandt and Abrassimov were described by their party, not their government, affiliations. See Neues Deutschland, June 20, 1968, p. 7. See also Der Spiegel, June 24, 1968, pp. 21 ff., and Peter Probst, "Neue DDR-Massnahmen im innerdeutschen Reiseverkehr," Deutschland Archiv 4 (1968).

10. Agreements between West Berlin and the GDR on visitors' passes (Passierscheine) were concluded on eight occasions between 1963 and 1966. In each case, West Berliners were allowed to visit East Berlin during a designated period of time, ranging from 14 to 19 days. Roughly 500,000 to 1.3 million West Berliners took advantage of the passes on these various occasions.

agreement than one limited to "an Easter Sunday stroll," and were reluctant to hold the presidential election elsewhere, it was the GDR that stood in the way of an agreement. Not only was East German propaganda considerably more vituperative than Soviet statements condemning the use of Berlin for official West German functions, but also the SED insisted more explicitly than the Soviets on the necessity of relocating the election as a precondition for any Passierschein agreement. The Berlin visitors' passes had become in effect a bargaining chip with which the GDR hoped to extract important political concessions from Bonn. Without a prior West German commitment to grant this concession, however, the GDR proved unresponsive to Soviet and West German requests for negotiations. After a first set of talks between the GDR and the West Berlin Senate foundered, the East Germans ignored all appeals for a second try. At one point, the Soviet ambassador in the Federal Republic, Zarapkin, flew to Chancellor Kiesinger's retreat to confer with him on the matter. Later, after the Soviet embassy advised the West Germans to contact the GDR in the expectation that last-minute talks could be initiated, the GDR made no response to Mayor Schuetz's soundings, a reaction that proved embarrassing to Moscow.11/

Ultimately, the electoral assembly met in West Berlin on March 5, in spite of Soviet and East German harassment of land and air traffic leading into the city. The upshot of this latest flap over Berlin, however, was that the SED leadership under Walter Ulbricht had magnified an existing controversy over the status of the city for the purpose of blocking the nascent process of detente that was now developing between the Soviet Union and the Federal Republic.

During the next two years, Ulbricht's efforts to halt, or at least retard, this process put him on a collision course with Soviet interests. Inevitably, Berlin figured as one of the most important items on the agenda of East-West detente. Foreign Minister Gromyko acknowledged as much in a speech to the Supreme Soviet of the USSR on July 10, 1969. Signalling Moscow's willingness to engage in discussions with Bonn and the three Western powers on a whole range of issues, Gromyko specifically noted that the Soviet Union was now ready for Four-power talks leading to the reduction of "complications" concerning the divided city. To the consternation of the GDR, the speech did not refer to West Berlin as an "independent political entity," which

---

11. See "Die Bonner Bereitschaft," Frankfurter Allgemeine Zeitung, March 4, 1969, p. 1, and Ernst-Otto Maetzke, "Bei Betrachtung einer Querlage," ibid.

was Ulbricht's preferred formulation, but merely to its "special status." Gromyko also refrained from placing West Berlin "on the territory" of the GDR, saying instead that it was located "in the heart of" the GDR, a juridically meaningless statement. The Soviet Foreign Minister also made mention of the "responsibilities" of the United States, Britain, and France concerning West Berlin, a fact of life which the East Germans generally preferred to ignore when militating for direct negotiations with the West Berlin Senate.12/

The East German regime promptly manifested its displeasure with the new Soviet signals. On July 16, a spokesman for the Foreign Ministry of the GDR declared that West Berlin was located "in the middle of the German Democratic Republic and on its territory," a new formula that underscored East Germany's sensitivities on the Berlin issue.13/ Later, in September, the delegates to the GDR's Volkskammer from East Berlin participated in the vote ratifying the nuclear Nonproliferation Treaty. This action, which violated the West's understanding that East Berlin was not a constituent part of the GDR, was a marked departure from the GDR's past adherence to a policy of not allowing the East Berlin delegation to take part in Volkskammer voting.14/

These early warnings of East Germany's unwillingness to go along with Soviet moves in the direction of an accommodation with the FRG were followed by similarly blatant expressions of opposition to the gathering momentum of Soviet-West German detente in 1970. At a wide-ranging press conference on January 19, Ulbricht astonished many of his listeners by asserting that there existed no residual Four-power authority over the GDR or over "the capital of the GDR, Berlin."15/ This remark seemed to be a rejoinder to a statement appearing in _Pravda_ four days earlier that reaffirmed the responsibility of the Four Powers for the resolution

---

12. For the text, see _Pravda_, July 11, 1969. Excerpts were also published in _Neues Deutschland_, July 11, 1969.

13. Ibid., July 17, 1969.

14. There is no direct evidence that the Soviets explicitly condoned this action. Ultimately, the SED did not succeed in permanently changing the voting status of the _Volkskammer_ delegates from East Berlin at this time. See articles in the _Frankfurter Allgemeine Zeitung_ by Detmar Cramer on February 4 and 7, 1969, and by B. Conrad in _Die Welt_, October 4, 1969.

15. _Neues Deutschland_'s coverage of the press conference was published on January 20 and 22, 1970.

of the German problem.16/ Several months later, as the Soviets pressured the GDR into beginning direct talks with the Brandt government, the SED used the Berlin issue to delay the start of this unprecedented inter-German dialogue. Originally, Brandt was to have met with his East German counterpart, Willi Stoph, in East Berlin. The SED scuttled this meeting, however, when Brandt divulged that he intended to make a stopover in West Berlin on his way back to Bonn. Agreement was reached on transferring the historic Brandt-Stoph encounter to Erfurt only after the GDR avoided efforts at finding a compromise for several days.

For the GDR, the commencement of the Four-power negotiations on Berlin on March 26, 1970, was surely one of the most disturbing elements of the evolving Soviet-West German rapprochement. As in other questions of paramount importance to the SED regime, such as its demand for _de jure_ recognition by Bonn and its concerns about excessive Soviet and East European economic dependence on the FRG, the Berlin issue loomed as an area in which compromises could be reached only at East Germany's expense. Virtually any significant Four-power agreement to normalize the Berlin situation would inevitably circumscribe the status of the GDR in matters pertaining to the city, diminish its ability to foment trouble on the access routes (with or without Soviet approval), and reduce its ability to bargain over such things as visitors' passes. Just as importantly, if the Soviets agreed to allow the "opening up" of the GDR to millions of West German visitors as part of an overall accommodation with the Federal Republic, Berlin would certainly become a major conduit for large numbers of West Germans desiring direct contacts with citizens of East Germany. For these reasons, it was in the interest of the Ulbricht regime to obstruct the conclusion of a Berlin accord.

As it happened, Ulbricht was at most able to delay, but not prevent, the Four-power agreement. The peak of Ulbricht's influence on the Soviet Union in this matter was apparently reached in late 1970 and early 1971. In the aftermath of the signature of the Soviet-FRG renunciation of force treaty on August 12, 1970, the SED launched an energetic campaign to convince the Brezhnev regime that Moscow was not sufficiently safeguarding vital GDR interests. By late November, the Soviets began to show greater sensitivity to Ulbricht's point of view. The Kremlin voiced support for East Germany's denunciation of the CDU/CSU's decision to hold a meeting of its Bundestag delegation in West Berlin at the end of the month, and at least did not veto the GDR's efforts

---

16. _Pravda_, January 15, 1970.

to block highway traffic to Berlin to back up this protest. On December 2, Ulbricht met with Brezhnev in East Berlin and reportedly told him that Moscow's policies validated China's recent claim that the Soviets were committing treason against the GDR. Stunned by Ulbricht's remonstrations, the Soviets, who had apparently hoped to convince the SED leader of the need to strike a compromise on Berlin, backed down. There then ensued an impasse in the Four-power talks, as Soviet negotiators accused the West of "ignoring the rights and sovereignty of the GDR," especially in the question of civilian traffic on the ground corridors leading to West Berlin.17/

The hardening of the Soviet negotiating posture at this juncture was not indicative of a complete about-face in Soviet policy, however. Rather it most probably represented a stalling tactic intended to give the Kremlin time to work out its difficulties with the GDR while maintaining a keen interest in reaching an agreement with the West. The Soviets were fully aware that progress on Berlin was essential to securing the ratification of the renunciation of force treaty by the Bundestag, no matter how often Soviet authorities might denounce this so-called "Berlin Junktim" in principle. Accordingly, the Soviets balanced their toughening attitudes with subtle indications of displeasure at Ulbricht's truculence.

It was only after Ulbricht's removal from office in May 1971, an action that was no doubt engineered by the Soviet Union, that the stalemate on Berlin was broken. The decisive breakthrough came in August, when the Soviet leadership, after several consultations with Honecker and his colleagues, suddenly showed signs of flexibility on the most disputed issues.18/ The resulting accord, signed by the Four Powers on September 3, violated Ulbricht's concerns on several key points. Most importantly, it confirmed Soviet, as opposed to East German, responsibility for traffic along the access routes to Berlin. It also allowed the Federal Republic to maintain and develop "ties" with West Berlin. Although the Soviets showed deference to East German sensibilities on these questions by asserting that the Quadripartite Agreement required the approval of the sovereign GDR, and by permitting the GDR to interpret the term "ties" more loosely than the Federal Republic (by using the word "Verbindungen" as opposed to "Bindungen"), it was clear that the agreement had been reached at the cost of significant concessions on the

____

17. Wettig, Conflict and Community, pp. 82-92.

18. Ibid., pp. 104 ff.

part of the GDR. While Honecker may very well have demurred at making these concessions, his personal authority was not as great as Ulbricht's, and having just gained power as a result of Soviet machinations, he was in no position to stand in the way of a Four-power settlement once it had been approved by Moscow.

THE GDR AND THE FUNCTIONS OF BERLIN SINCE 1971

What have been the principle results of ten years of detente for the GDR's position in Berlin? One way of approaching this question is to examine the three political functions referred to in the first part of this essay with a view to determining what role they have played in East German policy since the conclusion of the Quadripartite Agreement. We shall then turn our attention to the fourth function that Berlin has increasingly come to fulfill for the GDR over the past decade, i.e., its role as a source of economic benefits.

Berlin and the Legal Competence of the GDR

The Soviet commitment in the Four-power agreement to maintain responsibility for traffic along the access routes to West Berlin, together with Moscow's pledge to expedite such traffic, undoubtedly places severe limits on the GDR's ability to claim sovereignty over these passageways. Public East German claims to this effect have consequently diminished in frequency and stridency since the end of 1971. However, the decision of the Four Powers to agree to disagree about the legal status of Berlin itself, combined with the Quadripartite Agreement's provision that West Berlin is not part of the Federal Republic, has left the GDR ample room to reaffirm its positions with respect to the relationship between West Berlin and the FRG. "Berlin" is still regarded as the capital of the GDR, while "Westberlin" is described as having a "special status."19/ Although the GDR insists that it respects the Quadripartite Agreement's provisions regarding the Federal Republic's right to maintain its ties ("Verbindungen") with West Berlin, the East German regime categorically rejects what it sees as West German attempts to integrate West Berlin into the FRG. The GDR has consistently protested the FRG's efforts to include references to the "Land Berlin" in international treaties, and does not accept

---

19. See Harry Ott, "The Class Character of the German Democratic Republic's Foreign Policy," German Foreign Policy 9:3 (1972): 195.

the October 1973 ruling of the West German Federal Court which maintained that the FRG-GDR Basic Treaty was not incompatible with the West German constitution's inclusion of Berlin as an integral part of the Federal Republic.20/ For the same reasons, the GDR protested West Germany's decision to locate a Federal Environmental Office in West Berlin in 1974, as well as its efforts to include West Berlin in the activities of the European Community. The GDR also takes every opportunity to negotiate Berlin-related matters with the West Berlin Senate rather than with federal authorities.21/

Meanwhile, the GDR in recent years has acted to upgrade the legal status of Volkskammer delegates from East Berlin. In June 1979, a law was passed leaving open the possibility that, in the future, these delegates would be directly elected by the population rather than simply designated by the city council of East Berlin as in the past.22/ Two yearslater, the possibilities opened up by this legislation were realized when the Berlin delegation was included in the popular elections to the Volkskammer held on June 14, 1981.23/ While both of these moves wereviolations of the West's interpretations of the status of Berlin, there are grounds for regarding them as reactions to the FRG's endeavors to buttress its links with West Berlin. The 1979 law, for example, followed in the wake of East

---

20. For documentation of East German views on Berlin, see Das Vierseitige Abkommen ueber Berlin und seine Realisierung (Dokumente 1971-1977) (Berlin [East]: Staatsverlag der DDR, 1978). This volume, essentially a translation of a book first published in Moscow, is reviewed by Jochen Hellman in Deutsche Aussenpolitik 23:2 (1978): 31-36.

21. Examples of these agreements include the waste disposal agreements of 1974 and 1980; the agreement on mutual assistance in the event of accidents on the Spree River boundary between the two parts of the city (1975); and the agreement providing for the construction on the locks at Spandau in 1977.

22. "Gesetz ueber die Wahlen zu den Volksvertretungen der Deutschen Demokratischen Republik" of June 28, 1979, published in Gesetzblatt der DDR, Part I, 1979, p. 139. For an analysis, see Wolfgang Seiffert, "Anmerkungen zur Aenderung des Gesetzes ueber die Wahlen zu den Volksvertretungen der DDR," Deutschland Archiv, August, 1979, p. 792.

23. See Karl Wilhelm Fricke, "Die Wahlen zur 8. Volkskammer," Deutschland Archiv, July 1981, pp. 680-681.

German protests of Bonn's decision to send three members of the West Berlin Abgeordnetenhaus to the European Parliament, while the direct elections of Berlin Volkskammer delegates in 1981 came six months after a Soviet protest at the election of a West German political figure, Hans-Jochen Vogel, as Mayor of West Berlin, and barely weeks after another prominent FRG politician, Richard von Weizsaecker, replaced Vogel in that post.

Two significant aspects of these continuing legal disputes stand out. First, the GDR has tended since 1971 to align its positions on Berlin much more closely with the Soviet Union's posture than was the case during Ulbricht's years in power. Second, the protests which the GDR (and Moscow) have directed at the FRG for alleged violations of Berlin's status have generally not resulted in major stoppages of traffic on the access routes or in similarly tense confrontations such as those that often characterized the situation prior to the Quadripartite Agreement. To be sure, problems remain, and the West has had legitimate grounds to protest violations of its understanding of the treaty.24/ In 1974, for example, the GDR denied entry to an official of the Federal Environmental Office in West Berlin. (No other officials of this agency were blocked from entering West Berlin after this incident, however, following protests by the three Western Powers.) In August 1976, East German authorities refused to allow the passage of busses bringing members of the CDU/CSU youth organization to West Berlin on the grounds that this organization's alleged involvement with individuals seeking to flee the GDR constituted a misuse of the access routes. On somewhat similar grounds, the GDR since 1976 has denied access to approximately four out of every 10,000 persons seeking to enter the GDR or East Berlin. In spite of these actions, however, the opportunities available to the GDR for expanding controversies concerning the status of Berlin into sharp tests of will over access to the city have been dramatically reduced since the agreement's conclusion. Today some 18 million persons travel to and from West Berlin without hindrance every year.25/

---

24. For accounts of alleged violation of the Quadripartite Accord by the GDR and/or the USSR, see Ernst Levy's catalog in the Frankfurter Allgemeine Zeitung, June 3, 1976, p. 6, and Gunther van Well, "Die Teilnahme Berlins am internationalen Geschehen: ein dringender Punkt auf der Ost-West-Tagesordnung," Europa Archiv 20 (October 25, 1976): 647-656.

25. Zehn Jahre Deutschlandpolitik (Bonn: Bundesministerium fuer innerdeutsche Beziehungen, 1980), pp. 18-19.

According to East German sources, some 19 million West Berliners visited the GDR or East Berlin between 1972 and 1978.26/ In short, the Quadripartite Agreement has brought a significant reduction in the GDR's ability to back up its claims regarding its legal competence with respect to Berlin with roadblocks. This represents a major restriction on its foreign policy maneuverability, a fact that may be as welcome in Moscow as it is in Bonn.

Berlin as Crisis Point and as Bargaining Chip

By the same token, the Quadripartite Agreement, along with the atmosphere of detente surrounding it, has deprived the GDR of much of its ability to exploit Berlin's crisis potential. Once again, the Soviet commitment to permit unhindered access to West Berlin imposes sharp limits on the GDR's ability to foment crises over Berlin for the purpose of aggravating tensions with Bonn. In addition, the GDR has come to recognize that it has acquired over the years a major stake in detente with the Federal Republic (mostly for economic reasons, as noted below). Consequently, the SED under Honecker has had considerably less incentive than it had under Ulbricht to provoke problems over Berlin.

Frictions in the inter-German relationship continue to exist, however, and the GDR since 1971 has taken advantage of several legal perogatives in its possession in order to exert pressure on Bonn. One of the most effective of these measures centers on the GDR's right to set visa requirements and minimum currency exchange obligations on visitors to the GDR or East Berlin. In the fall of 1973, for example, the SED abruptly doubled the currency exchange requirement and extended their application to senior citizens. The move was regarded by many as intended mainly to reduce the number of Westerners visiting East Germany. Moreover, it served notice on the West German government that the GDR was not without mechanisms for creating difficulties for Bonn. Subsequent negotiations with the FRG, however, indicated that these measures were also adopted so as to improve the GDR's bargaining position vis-à-vis the Federal Republic. Following an exchange of letters with Chancellor Schmidt in September 1974, Honecker in October agreed to cut back the recent currency exchange obligation increase by two-thirds. Subsequently, the

----

26. Hellman, Deutsche Aussenpolitik: 33.

GDR restored the exemption from these exchange requirements previously accorded to older persons. These "concessions" opened the way for the successful negotiation of the "swing" credit arrangement, whereby the GDR has access to special credits from West Germany, and led to new agreements easing travel restrictions on citizens of West Berlin. The upshot of this episode was that both the FRG and the GDR had important bargaining chips to place on the negotiating table: while Bonn had money, the regime in East Berlin possessed sufficient legal mechanisms to curtail the flow of Western travelers into the GDR.

In October 1980, the GDR once again made use of its perogatives in this area by quadrupling the minimum exchange requirement and reimposing the exchange obligation on older citizens. This hefty increase in the amount of Western currency visitors must exchange for an equivalent amount of East German Marks (i.e., 25 DM) resulted in more than a fifty percent reduction in the number of persons passing from West Berlin into East Berlin.27/ To be sure, the East German authorities were probably anxious to limit the number of Westerners having contacts with East German citizens at a time of acute social turmoil in Poland, and were also probably interested in showing their pique at Chancellor Schmidt's cancellation of his planned meeting with Honecker in August. After a period of difficult bargaining, the GDR made several concessions, but these have been relatively minor in net effect. In exchange, the East Germans have received enormous guaranteed loans and other concessions from Bonn. It is clear that the GDR's ability to set these requirements provides it with the means to reduce the flow of traffic into the GDR, to demonstrate its disapproval of Bonn's policies, and, just as importantly, to obtain bargaining leverage in its dealings with the FRG.

Berlin's Economic Value to the GDR

One of the greatest changes in Berlin's relevance to the GDR since 1971 derives from its economic value to the East German regime. Although the presence in Berlin of the Treuhandstelle for trade between the two German states had helped channel the benefits of economic relations with the FRG to East Germany prior to the Grundlagenvertrag, it was only after 1971-72 that the GDR began to gain substantial economic advantages from the Federal Republic as a result of Berlin. As the government of the Federal Republic has sought to

---

27. The Washington Post, March 27, 1981.

reinforce East Germany's commitment to detente with strong economic incentives, Berlin has become the rationale for a number of inter-German accords involving generous West German outlays of cash.

In addition, West Berlin has been included in other agreements between the two German states which involve West German payments to the GDR such as the postal agreement of October 1977.28/ In April 1981, the GDR signaled its interest in starting talks with the West Berlin Senat on the S-Bahn system.29/ It subsequently agreed to transfer control of the West Berlin portion of this elevated rail system, thereby losing some presence in West Berlin, but gaining economically.

Meanwhile, trade between West Berlin and the GDR has risen appreciably in recent years. According to official East German statistics, total trade turnover between the GDR and West Berlin rose from 621.4 million VM in 1970 to over three million VM by 1983.30/ As shown in Table 8.1, the most dramatic rise in this trade occurred after the normalization of inter-German relations in 1972.

West German statistics tell the story of West Berlin's trade with the GDR and East Berlin as shown in Table 8.2. A comparison of the totals shown indicates that West Berlin's trade deficit with the GDR grew appreciably after 1970, reaching a figure of over 1 billion DM by 1980, as shown in Table 8.3.

Of particular significance to West Berlin consumers are the GDR's deliveries of food products, textiles, and clothing. Official West Berlin statistics indicate that the extent of these imports has risen significantly in recent years. By 1979, West Berlin was importing agricultural products (including plant products, forest products, game, live animals and, meat products) worth more than 166 million DM, in addition to approximately 10.5 million DM worth of textiles and 91.5 million DM worth of clothing.31/

---

28. For the text of the postal agreement, see _Zehn Jahre Deutschlandpolitik_, pp. 319-320.

29. The GDR proposed talks on the S-Bahn on April 27, 1981. On the GDR's problems with the West Berlin S-Bahn, see Gisela Helwig, "Streik bei der Reichsbahn," _Deutschland Archiv_, October 1980, pp. 1018-1019.

30. The Valuta-Mark (VM) is the GDR foreign trade currency. In 1978, 1 VM was equal to 0.634 DM.

31. Statistisches Landesamt Berlin, "Warenverkehr Berlins (West) mit dem uebrigen Bundesgebiet sowie mit der DDR und Ostberlin," 1980.

TABLE 8.1
Total GDR trade turnover with West Berlin

Year	Amount in Millions of Valuta-Marks
1970	621.4
1971	586.9
1972	685.2
1973	917.6
1974	1,087.4
1975	1,485.1
1976	1,919.5
1977	1,584.3
1978	1,643.2
1979	2,189.7
1980	2,771,7
1981	3,042.9
1982	3,151.6
1983	3,353.7

Source: Statistisches Jahrbuch der Deutschen Demo-kratischen Republic, volumes for 1979 through 1984.

TABLE 8.2
West Berlin's trade with the GDR[a]

Exports of Manufactured Goods to the GDR & East Berlin

	1970	1975	1976	1977	1978	1979	1980
Direct[b]	127	228	294	263	272	280	258
Indirect[c]	263	419	650	467	344	511	802
Total	490	747	944	730	616	791	1062

Imports of Manufactured Goods from the GDR & East Berlin

	1970	1975	1976	1977	1978	1979	1980
Direct[d]	396	801	993	1057	986	1360	1604
Indirect[e]	163	227	292	156	159	300	468
Total	559	1028	1285	1213	1145	1660	2072

[a]In million of DM; services not included
[b]Includes goods produced in West Berlin and exported to the GDR and East Berlin directly from West Berlin
[c]Includes goods produced in West Berlin and exported to the GDR via the Federal Republic
[d]Includes goods imported from the GDR by West Berlin and intended for use in the Federal Republic
[e]Includes goods imported from the GDR by West Berlin intended for use in the Federal Republic
Source: Bundesamt fuer gewerbliche Wirtschaft, Statistisches Landesamt Berlin. I am indebted to Caroline Ward for supplying these statistics.

TABLE 8.3
West Berlin's trade balance with the GDR[a]

	1970	1975	1976	1977	1978	1979	1980
Imports	559	1028	1285	1213	1145	1660	2072
Exports	490	747	944	730	616	791	1060
Deficit	69	281	341	483	529	869	1012

[a]Manufactured goods in millions DM, including both direct and indirect imports and exports
Source: Bundesamt fuer gewerbliche Wirtschaft, Statistisches Landesamt Berlin.

What all these figures suggest is that economic relations between West Berlin and the GDR are becoming increasingly profitable for both sides. Just as West Berlin is for the GDR both a source of supplies not as readily (or as cheaply) available elsewhere, and a convenient market for consumer agricultural products and manufactures, West Berlin for its part benefits from the profits and employment opportunities that accrue from doing business with the GDR and from the relatively inexpensive food products, clothing, and other items exported by the GDR. To this must be added, on the one hand, advantages such as the waste disposal facilities which the GDR has agreed to make available to West Berlin, and on the other, the large amounts of hard currency which the GDR obtains from foreign visitors visiting from West Berlin.32/

At the same time, however, it is apparent that this mutually advantageous economic relationship is by no means indispensable for either West Berlin or the GDR. The share which their reciprocal trade occupies in the total trading patterns of the two sides is still too small to permit one to speak of genuine interdependence in their economic relations.33/ Even when one considers the fact that more than 30 percent of West Berlin's imports come from the GDR, it is doubtful that a cutoff of these imports would seriously threaten the life of the city. Thus, although both the GDR and West Berlin benefit from their trade, both could survive without it if necessary.

THE GDR AND BERLIN: A BALANCE SHEET

What conclusions may be drawn from this overview of the GDR's involvement in Berlin, and more specifically, what have been the positive and negative effects of the

---

32. In addition to the hard currency flowing into the East German treasury from visa charges and currency exchange requirements, foreigners are allowed to give East German citizens cash gifts. Much of this money is then eventually spent in special shops carrying "luxury" items in the GDR.

33. In 1979, trade with the GDR accounted for approximately 13.4 percent of West Berlin's total exports and 30.3 percent of its imports. In the same year, trade with West Berlin amounted to about two percent of the GDR's total trade turnover, but 25.1 percent of its combined trade with the FRG and West Berlin. Computed from figures provided by the Statistisches Landesamt Berlin and the Statistisches Taschenbuch der DDR, 1980.

stabilization of the Berlin situation on the GDR in the last ten years? To put the answers to these questions in a broader context, it may also be fitting to ask how the GDR would deal with West Berlin if it could have its ultimate wish. In the best of all possible worlds (from the GDR leadership's point of view), would the SED act to incorporate West Berlin into the GDR or might it prefer some other solution? Finally, considering that the GDR must accommodate its preferences to political realities, how is the GDR likely to treat the Berlin issue in the foreseeable future?

Clearly there has been a mixture of gains and losses over Berlin for the GDR in the past fifteen years. On balance, however, it is questionable whether the gains which the GDR has acquired as a result of the stabilization of Berlin outweigh the disadvantages.

Certainly on the question of sovereign rights and the ability to exercise them, the GDR came up with less on Berlin than it would have liked. Instead of gaining undisputed legal authority over the access routes, as Khrushchev once promised Ulbricht, the GDR was forced to accept Moscow's reaffirmation of Soviet responsibility for access to West Berlin. Furthermore, the Quadripartite Agreement has also hampered the GDR's ability to foment trouble by arbitrarily hindering traffic bound for West Berlin from the FRG. While the continuing East-West wrangling over the formal status of Berlin, and the Quadripartite Agreement's provision that West Berlin is not part of the FRG, provide the GDR with grounds for protesting West German activities in West Berlin (or, as noted earlier, for occasionally barring access to certain categories of West Germans), the GDR's room for maneuver is considerably narrower in this domain than it was before 1971.

On the positive side, the most important item that remains in the GDR's diminished arsenal of foreign policy initiatives with respect to Berlin is its ability to fix visa fees, currency exchange requirements, and the like. While these measures may be used to discourage West Germans from visiting the GDR, past experience has shown that the GDR has been willing to reach compromises on these matters for the sake of coming to terms with the FRG on economic or other agreements. As a result, the GDR's capacity to engage in practices of this kind has developed into a form of bargaining chip that provides the East German leadership with at least a modicum of leverage in its transactions with the Federal Republic.

To be sure, the GDR has also reaped substantial economic rewards as a result of a host of agreements with West Germany in which Berlin plays a prominent role. Conceivably, the GDR's stake in agreements of this sort, as well as in trade with West Berlin, could increase markedly in coming years. Even here, however, there are inherent limits on the importance of these economic benefits as they might be viewed by the SED. For one thing, the East German leadership knows that Bonn's willingness to channel large sums of money into highway construction, road tolls and similar aspects of <u>Berlin-Verkehr</u> is in part dependent on "good behavior" by the GDR, not only in the Berlin question, but also over the whole range of issues affecting inter-German relations. In this way, Bonn, too, has significant bargaining chips that can be used to apply pressure on the GDR in matters relating to Berlin. Thus, the economic gains the GDR has received as a result of the stabilization of the situation have not been without a political cost.

Moreover, it is worth asking just how much the GDR actually values the large sums of money it has accumulated in consequence of stabilization. To be sure, this is a matter that the GDR authorities must judge for themselves. While these amounts are by no means inconsiderable and may be especially welcome at a time of economic stringency in the GDR,<u>34/</u> it is not likely that the GDR regime regards them as indispensable to the successful functioning of the East German economy. Thus, it is possible to imagine situations in which the GDR's economic stake in the maintenance of political quiescence over Berlin may be perceived by the SED as not worth the disadvantages that emanate from the presence of an outpost of Western (and, indeed, West German) society some 110 miles inside East German territory.

Meanwhile, the potential dangers to the stability of the East German regime stemming from West Berlin continue to be substantial and have even increased since the normalization of relations with the Federal Republic. As in the past, West Berlin continues to function as a transmitter of news and culture from the West via radio and television broadcasts beamed into East German households. More importantly, West Berlin up to 1980 has been the entry point for over three million travelers annually streaming into East Berlin from the West. While the numbers of these visitors has declined since then, they are arguably still high enough to be regarded as constituting a serious risk for the SED leadership. Moreover, the reestablishment of direct dialing procedures between East and West Berlin in 1976

---

34. On the political implications of the GDR's current economic predicament, see Michael J. Sodaro, "External Influences on Regime Stability in the GDR: A Linkage Analysis," in <u>Foreign and Domestic Policy in Eastern Europe in the 1980s</u>, eds. Michael J. Sodaro and Sharon L. Wolchik (New York: St. Martin's, 1983).

132

has greatly expanded the number of telephone conversations between Berliners on either side of the wall.
Although the enhanced opportunities for direct
communications between citizens of the two Germanies may
not result in real social upheaval in the GDR, at the
very least they help keep alive the notion of national
unity among Germans, thus detracting from whatever
popular acceptance to SED regime may possess.35/
That the current SED leadership under Honecker is
sensitive to these considerations is indicated by the
hard bargaining position the GDR maintained under great
pressure from Bonn (wielding both carrot and stick) to
return to the pre-1980 status quo.

The SED has also been troubled by the activities of
West German journalists in East Germany. Following the
initial normalization agreements between the Federal
Republic and the GDR, West German print and broadcast
media journalists were given greater freedom to operate
in the GDR. Television reporters took advantage of the
new latitude by staging "man-in-the-street" interviews
in East Berlin, often with embarrassing results for the
SED authorities. A crackdown followed in 1979 as the
GDR passed stiff new laws restricting the functions of
Western news gatherers.36/ In addition, the regime has
expelled particular journalists for reporting stories
unfavorable to the GDR. Although this issue belongs to
the broader category of relations between the GDR and
the Federal Republic, and is not confined to Berlin, the
instant access that West Berlin affords to journalists
covering events in East Berlin certainly aggravates the
problem for the GDR.

Similarly, West Berlin aggravates the difficulties
that exiled East German dissidents have caused the GDR
in recent years. Even since Wolf Biermann was stripped
of his GDR citizenship after being allowed to travel to
the FRG in 1976, there has been a westward exodus of
writers, artists, performers and other prominent members
of the GDR's cultural and intellectual elite. Many of
them have gravitated to West Berlin, and some have been
allowed to retain visa rights enabling them to make
return visits to the GDR. While to a certain extent the
SED's policy of actively encouraging a number of these
critics of the regime to leave the GDR has acted as a

---

35. A poll of East German youth reportedly conducted by
the SED indicated that 75 percent of those aged 16 to 25
thought of themselves as "Germans," not East Germans.
Der Spiegel, October 1, 1979.

36. For the new restrictions on journalists, see Neues
Deutschland, April 14-15, 1979.

"safety valve," allowing the GDR to get rid of potential troublemakers, the long-term effects of this emigration may prove debilitating for the GDR. The books, interviews, and other works published by these dissidents after they reach the West may ultimately find their way to East German readers, posing potentially serious problems for the SED in dealing with the East German intellectual elite.37/ Indeed, some former GDR dissidents who now reside in West Germany have explicitly announced their intention of trying to reform East Germany through intellectual and political action in the West. Such is the avowed aim of a segment of the leftist _Alternativen_ in West Berlin, a group that in 1984 strongly outpolled the SED's sister party in West Berlin, the ineffectual SEW.

In each of these foregoing areas, Berlin acts to intensify problems that are already part and parcel of West Germany's general cultural penetration of the GDR. What this balance sheet suggests, however, is that the SED still has ample reason to regard the existence of West Berlin with a certain uneasiness. If present realities were somehow suspended and the East German leadership could be granted its greatest desire, it most probably would prefer to see the Western presence in Berlin eliminated and West Berlin incorporated into the GDR. Since there is virtually no possibility that such an outcome will occur in the foreseeable future, however, the likelihood is that Berlin will increasingly become for the GDR a bargaining device to be used in its dealings with Bonn. Thus, the GDR will employ its visa and currency exchange policies, its control over Western journalists, and the like, as bargaining chips designed to influence Bonn's political and economic relationships with East Germany. At the same time, Bonn will use its own bargaining levers with respect to Berlin to induce the GDR to adopt favorable policies towards the Federal Republic.

To be sure, both the GDR and the Soviet Union will continue to adhere to their strict interpretation of the Federal Republic's ties with West Berlin, and disputes with the West over this issue are not likely to disappear. Indeed, a measure of conflict is necessary to maintain Berlin's utility as a bargaining chip. The intensity of these disputes, however, will in all probability remain at a relatively low key (as they have since 1971) as long as both the Soviets and the East Germans see a value in renewed detente with the Federal Republic, if not with the West as a whole. (In fact,

---

37. On GDR dissenters, see Michael J. Sodaro, "Limits to Dissent in the GDR: Fragmentation, Cooptation and Repression," in _Dissent in Eastern Europe_, ed. Jane L. Curry (New York: Praeger, 1983), pp. 82-116.

good relations with Bonn are essential to permitting the Soviets to encourage Bonn to influence United States policy towards Moscow.) Any major breech of the Quadripartite Agreement would certainly represent a blow to any prospect for a renewal of detente between East and West. The future of Berlin in East-West relations appears secure. More than at any other time in the past, Berlin will be an object of mutual bargaining and leverage-seeking rather than a source of crisis in itself.

Prospects for Berlin:
Economic and Social Trends

9

West Berlin and the Two Germanies: The Interplay of Political and Economic Motives

Ronald A. Francisco

The governments of West Berlin and the Federal Republic of Germany (FRG) have long sought to preserve West Berlin's economic vitality. Berlin is surrounded by the German Democratic Republic (GDR) and is closer to Poland than to West Germany. The GDR has capitalized on this spatial isolation in order to pressure West Berlin and its citizens. It has been uncooperative and has created significant obstacles for communication, all in the hope that a severely isolated West Berlin could not endure in the long term.

Since the late 1970s, however, the amount of GDR interaction with West Berlin has increased considerably. West Berlin leaders, too, have shown surprising initiative and independence in dealing with the GDR. While these developments signal a positive trend, they do not likely represent a fundamental shift in policy. This chapter argues that the increase in West Berlin-GDR trade and cooperation provides needed relief from many of the economic difficulties that burden the GDR, while at the same time bolstering the prospects of West Berlin.

The leaders of West Berlin and the FRG have placed considerable emphasis on this development. West Berlin's governing mayor Eberhard Diepgen has even underscored publicly the importance of structured cooperation: "For West Berlin there are two links (Verklammerungen): One the incorporation in the Western alliance and the other to the GDR."1/ Erich Honecker and the rest of the East German leadership are plainly skeptical about any long-term ties to the West. Yet their motivation is not wholly unlike Diepgen's. Both the GDR and West Berlin face an array of difficult economic problems.

Predictions about the future of Berlin are

---

1. "Diepgen: Westberlin Klammer zur DDR," <u>Sueddeutsche Zeitung</u>, July 9, 1984, p. 2.

137

precarious. A simple extrapolation of present trends, however, indicates that objective needs are likely to lead the GDR and West Berlin to continued economic cooperation within a context of general discord.

The relationship between the GDR and West Berlin is governed, as this volume makes clear, by a complex web of interests and alliances. Resulting demands create significant obstacles to cooperation: West Berlin must remain under Four-power protection and must stress its inherent legal and political ties to the Federal Republic. The GDR must emphasize the independence of West Berlin and must remain loyal above all to the USSR.

These mutually incompatible goals led for decades to a level of discord and delimitation that approached absurdity. Now, however, events have transformed these same orientations to the extent that they encourage interaction and cooperation.

THE GERMAN DEMOCRATIC REPUBLIC

Erich Honecker stated unequivocally in 1983 that the GDR would not succumb to economic pressure: "The German Democratic Republic is not prepared to agree to any package in the development of its trade and economic relations that includes political demands."2/ However strongly Honecker and his colleagues hold this view, it amounts to little more than wishful thinking. Almost any arrangement with the Federal Republic is indirectly linked to some expectation of a political or human rights concession. While these have appeared paltry from the West, to the GDR leadership they represent embarrassing surrenders of sovereignty. Even when the GDR seeks to avoid this problem by dealing with other Western nations it is confronted with demands for reparations and other concessions. Why does the GDR tolerate this interference? Given its debt, energy, and technology problems, it has little choice.

The Burden of Debt

The GDR has borrowed heavily over the preceding decade in order to finance its trade deficits, acquire technology, and satisfy its demanding citizenry. The debt is large and multifaceted. It has four primary components: (1) convertible currency debt to the West; (2) trade and direct currency debt to the FRG; (3) trade

---

2. Quoted in "In Handelsfragen kein politisches Junktim," _Frankfurter Allgemeine Zeitung_, November 5, 1983, p. 4.

debt to the USSR in transferable rubles; and (4) convertible currency obligations through the CMEA's International Investment Bank.

The need for Western currency has grown problematic for the GDR. Normally considered a cautious and defensive government, it was forced to reckless levels of borrowing. By 1984 it had virtually no credit rating with Western banks. It was rescued in this instance by massive West German loans.3/ At the cost of distasteful political concessions the GDR transferred much of its Western bank debt to more liberal West German government-guaranteed credits. Since then, the East Germans have gone back to the international banking community for more loans.

Table 9.1 indicates the development of the GDR's Western debt and its consequent debt-service burden. The table does not include the special West German "swing" credits and other West German-guaranteed debt. These official FRG loans amounted to over DM one billion in 1984 alone.4/ The "swing" loans allow interest-free access to inter-German trade. They must be repaid, but are estimated to save the GDR over $31 million in interest payments annually.5/ The GDR thus has a capitalist benefactor that Poland, Rumania, and other hard-pressed CMEA states must envy. Yet the GDR has recently sought loans from Japanese and American banks in order to elude the FRG's inevitable demands for political concessions.6/

The GDR also faces a less burdensome, but quite real debt to the Soviet Union. It is estimated at 3.5 million transferable rubles. It stems from the GDR's frequent trade deficits with the USSR and from a program installed by the Soviets a decade ago. The Soviet Union required its CMEA allies to invest in raw material projects in the USSR. This has been a double burden for the GDR. First, Moscow tired of paying all of the research, equipment, and production costs for oil, gas

---

3. See Roger Pine, "Uneasy Western Banks Pulling Back on Loans," Wall Street Journal, July 1, 1982, pp. 1 and 10; also Paul Legg, "West Germany's Detente Policy Boomerangs," ibid., September 11, 1985, p. 31.

4. "DM-Devisen an die DDR (1984)," Die Zeit, July 20, 1984, p. 4.

5. "Credit Aids Inter-German Ties," Wall Street Journal, July 25, 1985, p. 21.

6. "East Germans Benefit from U.S. Bank Credits That Don't Call for Human-Rights Concessions," Wall Street Journal, March 19, 1985, p. 36.

TABLE 9.1
East German Debt and Debt-Service Obligation to the West

	1973	1975	1977	1979	1980
Gross:[a]	2,136	5,188	7,145	10,912	14,410
Net:[b]	1,876	3,548	6,195	8,950	9,700
Debt-Service Ratio (percent):	25	27	40	40	60

	1981	1982	1983	1984	1985
Gross:	14,860	13,040	10,500	9,000	10,000
Net:	11,900	10,100	8,000	6,500	6,000
Debt-Service Ratio (percent):	60	50	40	35	35

[a]Total debt in millions of U.S. dollars; does not include obligations to the West German government.

[b]Gross net minus GDR deposits in Western banks.

Sources: U.S. Central Intelligence Agency, Handbook of Economic Statistics, 1981, p. 41; Paul Marer, "East European Economies," in Communism in Eastern Europe, eds. T. Rakowska-Harmstone and A. Gyorgy (Bloomington: Indiana University Press, 1979), p. 277; Roger Thurow, "East Germany to Get Credit," Wall Street Journal, July 26, 1984, p. 29; David R. Francis, "West European Bankers Breathe Easier Over Loans to East Bloc," Christian Science Monitor, October 16, 1984, p. 23; Amity Shales, "Soviet Bloc Economies," Wall Street Journal, March 1, 1984; "East European Debt," The Economist, August 31, 1985, p. 90; "A Comecon Exemplar," The Economist, July 6, 1985, p. 64.

and other resource development. Hence, the GDR is required to divert its already meager investment resources to the Soviet Union, away from its own planned technology development. Second, the USSR requires all CMEA members to assume proportional shares of its Western energy-development debt through the CMEA's International Investment Bank. The East Germans must pay a portion of this Soviet-contracted debt, and they must pay in scarce convertible currency at world market rates of interest.7/

It is difficult to see how the GDR can extricate itself from this cycle of debt and international dependence. It has little bargaining power with the USSR, particularly with its higher living standards. Those same living standards depend upon continued imports of consumer goods, technology, and energy from the West, all of which require Western funds. It is unlikely that the GDR leadership wishes to run the political risk of severe austerity in the consumer sector.

Energy

Measured in terms of raw energy dependence, the GDR's 30 percent shortfall amounts to less than half of West Germany's burden in securing an adequate annual supply of energy. Yet the GDR is far less capable of operating on international markets, and energy is therefore a problematic sector for the Honecker regime.

The problems have been exacerbated by the Soviet Union's own disappointments in the energy field. The GDR was once wholly dependent on Soviet oil, supplied on lenient, soft-currency terms. The GDR was beginning to wean itself from the USSR when the international situation changed drastically. While the GDR cheered the Arab oil embargo against the United States and its allies, the consequent quadrupling of oil prices shocked Eastern Europe as well. The GDR was faced with sharply increased payments for Arab crude oil. The Soviets then delivered the unhappy news that they would begin limiting increases in exports and would institute a new pricing system.

These tidings could hardly have come at a worse time. The GDR's hard coal reserves were nearly exhausted, and the nation was short of essential raw materials such as coking coal, coke, oil, and non-

---

7. Paul Marer, "East European Economies: Achievements, Problems, Prospects," in Communism in Eastern Europe, eds. T. Rakowska-Harmstone and A. Gyorgy (Bloomington: Indiana University Press, 1979), p. 269.

142

ferrous metals.8/ Although the Soviets were able to
increase their oil deliveries to Eastern Europe
throughout the 1970s, they began to reduce exports to
the GDR in 1982. The GDR's need to secure oil on world
markets increased to perhaps 20 to 30 percent of its
total oil imports--all for Western currency.

Meanwhile, the Soviets continued to hold to a
pricing regime that had been established in 1975. Prices
were adjusted annually on the basis of a five-year
moving average of world oil prices. The GDR's exposure
to this pricing system added incrementally to the GDR's
financial and energy burdens. As a result of the Soviet
policy, all CMEA states (except Rumania) moved from
surplus to deficit status in the bilateral Soviet trade
balance after 1975.

The GDR found it difficult to adapt to these new
circumstances. It had committed the nation in 1971 to a
large increase in private automobiles and a switch from
electric to diesel locomotives. After 1973 it adopted a
crash program to build nuclear power plants and imposed
Draconian recycling and conservation policies. It was
forced to reduce the amount of oil that could be used
for heating. By 1983 only 25 percent of all oil could be
burned for heating, and in 1984 a decree forbade any use
of oil for space heating.9/

By 1983 it had become clear that the GDR could not
reduce further its dependence on foreign energy. The GDR
leadership decided to pressure the Soviets to reduce
their price for oil. The 37th meeting of the CMEA was
held in East Berlin in October 1983. As hosts, the East
Germans cautiously pointed out that the Soviet pricing
structure had made Soviet oil and gas about ten percent
more expensive than current world market prices.10/ The
appeal, joined by other East European states, led the
Soviets to arrange an extraordinary meeting of the CMEA
in Moscow the following June. There it was announced
that the Soviet price for oil would henceforth be "more
flexibly adjusted to world market prices"--for a price:

---

8. U.S. Central Intelligence Agency, Energy Supplies in
Eastern Europe (1979), p. 1; and National Basic Intelligence Factbook (1978), p. 73.

9. Theo Sommer, "1984 wird unser bestes Jahr," Die Zeit,
August 3, 1984, p. 3; for a complete analysis, see
Wolfgang Stinglwagner, Die Energiewirtschaft der DDR
(Bonn: Gesamtdeutsches Institut, 1985), especially pp.
180-200.

10. "Die Ostblocklaender wollen wirtschaftlich enger
zusammenruecken," Frankfurter Allgemeine Zeitung, October 21, 1983, p. 2.

The East Europeans promised in exchange to provide the USSR with "required goods of high quality and world technological levels."11/

These new arrangements may restore a higher level of Soviet oil exports and, given falling oil prices, surely reduce the costs of energy imports. Nonetheless, the fact that the GDR must now provide more finished, technologically sophisticated goods to the USSR might reduce its ability to export to the West for convertible currency. It may also reveal the GDR's growing problems in sustaining technological innovation.

Technological Weakness

The new Soviet demands for technology fall most heavily on the GDR. For the whole of its existence, the GDR has played the role of premier technological innovator in the CMEA and key supplier to the USSR. While the GDR still enjoys this reputation, it is now based far more on the nation's unique access to Western markets and its extensive industrial espionage system.12/ The GDR has been unable to keep up with the West in independent technological development.

The East Germans are caught in a frustrating cycle of dependence. It must import Western technology in order to minimize the deterioration of its position and to supply its restive population. But this requires the sale of its exports in Western markets to offset the costs of these purchases. Yet precisely because it lacks modern technology, the GDR has difficulty producing competitive goods for Western markets.13/

Nor is the GDR able to maintain its once vaunted role as a supplier of critical technology to the Soviet Union. The Soviets are painfully aware of the CMEA's lagging technological development. Increasingly, they seek their new production machinery in the West. In the early 1950s, the GDR provided 43 percent of the Soviet Union's total machinery purchases. By 1965, the figure had declined to 28 per cent, and by the late 1970s it

---

11. Bernhard Kueppers, "Erhoehte Ausprueche Moskaus an die Partner," Sueddeutsche Zeitung, June 18, 1984, p. 4.

12. Frederick Kempe, "Silicon Satellites," Wall Street Journal, September 16, 1985, p. 76C.

13. See Pedro Ramet, "Disaffection and Discontent in East Germany," World Politics 37:1 (October 1984): 107-109.

144

was only 17 per cent.14/ In the 1980s the Soviets have reversed traditional roles. They sell large quantities of machinery, electronic data processing and audio equipment to the GDR.

In order to arrest the deterioration, the GDR embarked on an aggressive program to acquire Western technology and to develop its own. The 1981-1985 plan gave high priority to the purchase of high-technology production machinery from the West in order to bolster the GDR's ability to compete in the consumer goods sector. During 1981 and 1982 East Germany purchased large orders of engineering, chemical, electrical, and electronic equipment from the West.

The GDR had intended to finance these imports by countertrading steel, plastics, fertilizer, and optical equipment. It failed, however, to sell to the West in the magnitude it envisioned. By 1983 its Western debt service obligations had become a serious problem. Along with other East European states, the GDR sharply curtailed Western imports and aggressively sought Western markets for its products.15/ While successful in the short term, this strategy does little to extricate the GDR from its cycle of technological and economic dependence on the West. Fewer Western imports mean less new technology; more Western exports require greater energy imports and discrimination against domestic economic sectors.

Even this state of affairs would not have been possible without the benevolence of the Federal Republic of Germany through its credits of 1983 and 1984 and its annual "swing" loan programs. The GDR's own course of action reflects little gratitude. Most of its estimated one thousand industrial spies operate in the Federal Republic and save the GDR some $1.7 billion in research and development costs.16/ The ideas gleaned from abroad are merged with the GDR's own research and implemented in the extensive system of decentralized Kombinate (a vertically integrated industrial sector).17/ For

---

14. Jochen Bethkenhagen, "Energieprobleme in der Sowjet-union und die Auswirkungen auf die wirtschaftlichen Entwicklungen in den osteuropaeischen Laendern," (Berlin [West]: Deutsches Institut fuer Wirtschaft, 1980), p. 400.

15. See for example "Eastern Promise," The Economist, December 1, 1984, p. 2.

16. "Industrial Espionage," The Economist, September 21, 1985, p. 70.

17. See Raymond Bentley, Technological Change in the

example, the GDR recently established an independent Kombinat for robotics research.18/

Additional help may come in the form of joint ventures with West German and West European firms. Nonetheless, the harsh fact remains that the GDR cannot compete on a world market level, cannot supply the USSR's technological appetite from its own resources, and cannot even provide a competitive lifestyle for its citizens, who must still wait 8 to 12 years for an automobile. It appears certain that the GDR will be forced to rely on its Western neighbor for the foreseeable future.

WEST BERLIN

West Berlin's economic problems are a product of geography and politics. They are too complex to be chronicled here.19/ This section focuses instead on the impressive recent arrest of West Berlin's economic decline and on a surprisingly independent spirit shown by Berlin's political leadership. Both of these, if they last, have important implications for the city and for relations with the GDR in the future.

Many families left Berlin during the city's rocky and risk-laden postwar history. Many of the young people moving the other way--i.e., to Berlin--were primarily interested in escaping from compulsory military service. As low-skill, less desirable jobs went unfilled, increasingly large numbers of foreign workers entered the city. The net result of these demographic trends was an increasingly old population with a youthful core of politicized radicals and a growing influx of Turks and other foreigners. Businesses began to abandon the city in greater numbers, and there was real concern for West Berlin's long-term viability.

In 1970 the federal government in Bonn embarked on

German Democratic Republic (Boulder: Westview Press, 1984).

18. "Milliarden-Kredit foerdert den DDR-Handel nicht," Sueddeutsche Zeitung, August 27, 1984, p. 15.

19. For a more complete view, see Gerhard Mensch, "Economic Perspectives for Berlin," in The Future of Berlin, ed. Martin J. Hillenbrand (Montclair, NJ: Allanheld, Osmun, 1980), pp 153-228; and Wolfgang Watter, "The West Berlin Economy," in Living with the Wall: West Berlin 1961-1985, eds. R.L. Merritt and A.J. Merritt (Durham, NC: Duke University Press, 1985), pp. 136-139.

a program of support for Berlin. Of course the FRG had always aided Berlin through its horizontal equalization system, but now it sought specifically to shore up the infrastructure of the economy. It offered special tax and other policy incentives to Berlin businesses. While it was a noble effort, Berlin's economy continued to deteriorate through the 1970s, with large employment losses.[20]/

The situation grew worse during the first years of the 1980s, when young radicals gained wide publicity with protests and building occupations. At the same time, Berlin trade unions outraged the Senate by impeding the free transit of goods from West Berlin to the FRG during a work stoppage.[21]/ Given the island city's history of blockades and general harassment, the unions trod on very sensitive and salient ground.

In the meantime, Berlin's new political leadership began to display optimism and creativity laced with a strong dose of realism. Governing mayor Richard von Weizsaecker rejected the notion that Berlin could ever be a "normal" city. He decided that Berlin's economic problems required solutions that matched their causes. No longer would federal subsidies alone be seen as most instrumental, despite the fact that they still amount to almost one-half of Berlin's annual budget.[22]/

Von Weizsaecker (now president of the Federal Republic) quickly took actions that were unprecedented for Berlin mayors. One of the most dramatic of these was a visit to the GDR. This action caused worry and consternation in Bonn, since it played into the hands of the GDR, who argue that West Berlin is an independent political entity, not linked to Bonn.[23]/

Von Weizsaecker and his successor Eberhard Diepgen have followed this aggressive path with considerable short-term success. Berlin began to work actively to recruit investment capital. Money and new businesses flowed in increasing volume to the city in the years

---

20. "Berlin braucht neue Arbeitsplaetze," _Sueddeutsche Zeitung_, August 4-5, 1984, p. 33.

21. "Oxfort: Behinderung des Berlinverkehrs 'instinktlos'," _Frankfurter Allgemeine Zeitung_, October 11, 1983, p. 1.

22. See Joachim Nawrocki, "In Berlin darf nichts wegbrechen," _Die Zeit_, December 17, 1982, pp. 7-9.

23. See Peter Jochen Winters, "Weizsaeckers Fehler beginnt sich zu raechen," _Frankfurter Allgemeine Zeitung_, October 27, 1983, p. 12.

that followed._24_/ There are presently six venture capital firms working in Berlin alone._25_/

West Berlin's economic performance in 1984 outstripped the Federal Republic's in every category. There were 6,000 more job openings at the end of the year, with growth still continuing. The old federal tax incentives were cited as least important in attracting this investment and growth. Businesses instead sought Berlin's "good location" (from a transport perspective), business networking, qualified workers, and excellent cooperation with institutions and universities._26_/

Table 9.2 shows several of the positive trends that have characterized the past several years. One of the more significant of these is trade with the GDR. From 1975 to 1983 West Berlin's trade with its neighbor increased by more than 112 percent (versus 87 percent for the Federal Republic)._27_/ The GDR's self-imposed import austerity in 1984 curtailed trade somewhat, but it began to rebound strongly in 1985.

While Berlin's economy continues to do well, there is no guarantee that this trend will endure. Indeed, the persistent problem of structural unemployment poses a significant challenge to Berlin's leadership. Nonetheless, the city has embarked on new and different course that seems to reflect not only its own special interests and potentials, but the interdependence that it shares with the GDR as well.

THE GROWTH OF INTERDEPENDENCE

The domestic and international problems of West Berlin and GDR have led in recent years to increased levels of interaction and interdependence. The Federal Republic of Germany plays a major role for both parties, and the GDR is in no way enthusiastic about this situation. It has actively sought loans from Japan and the

---

24. See "Berlin wird wieder attraktiver," _Stuttgarter Zeitung_, March 2, 1983, p. 16; "Berlinfoerderung kaum von Einfluss," _Frankfurter Allgemeine Zeitung_, March 6, 1984, p. 11; or "Berlin spart und investiert," ibid., October 12, 1983, p. 4.

25. "In Berin wird Risiko-Kapital gesammelt," _Sueddeutsche Zeitung_, August 4-5, 1984, p. 24.

26. Michael Jungblut, "Wende-Probe an der Spree," _Die Zeit_, March 8, 1985, p. 11.

27. Calculated from _Statistisches Jahrbuch der DDR_ (Berlin [East]: Staatsverlag, 1984), p. 237.

TABLE 9.2
West Berlin's economic performance and trade with the GDR

	1981	1982	1983	1984	1985[a]
Orders:[b]	+1	-4	+5	+8	+7
Production:	+1	-3	+5	+7	+4
Trade with GDR:					
Exports:	+13	-12	+21	-21	+17
Imports:	+12	+11	-4	+6	-3

[a]Includes data from January and February only.

[b]These and all data in the table in the form of percentage change calculated on an annual basis.

Source: Adapted from "Die Berliner Wirtschaft in Zahlen," Die Berliner Wirtschaft, 1981 issues through issue of May 17, 1985.

United States in order to avoid West German demands. It
even managed to gain terms of trade with Austria that
enabled the GDR to buy substantial amounts of tech-
nology.28/ In practical terms, however, it is impossible
for the GDR to escape substantial dependence on the
Federal Republic.

The GDR

     Ironically, it is in large measure because of
Soviet demands that the East Germans must continue to
negotiate with the FRG. The Soviet Union's 1984 demands
for increased technology shipments coincided with an
insistence that the GDR increase its military spending.
The Soviet Union is unlikely to resume complete coverage
of GDR energy needs and will almost certainly continue
its requirement that the GDR repay its transferable
ruble and convertible currency debts within the CMEA.
     These demands force the GDR to look westward. It
alone enjoys tariff-free access to the EEC among all
CMEA members. Only the GDR has a willing, even self-
sacrificing benefactor to save it from crushing debt
obligations. And the GDR certainly has the easiest and
most direct access to joint ventures and other technology transfer mechanisms.
     The Volkswagen Corporation agreed in 1984 to a
joint venture with the GDR for the manufacture of
engines on a subcontracting basis.29/ These kinds of
arrangements are very beneficial to the GDR. They are
becoming more numerous and will likely continue to grow.
Ever mindful of the political baggage that accompanies
pacts with the FRG, the GDR has sought to conclude joint
arrangements elsewhere.30/ Yet it is difficult to see
any large potential for the GDR anywhere but in the
Federal Republic and West Berlin.
     Perhaps the best single example of the changing
political and economic environment in Germany is the
GDR's sale of the S-Bahn. The S-Bahn, an elevated railway, remained under GDR control in West Berlin after the
division of the city. It represented a symbol of
official access for the GDR to West Berlin, as well as a
source of needed Western currency. But a boycott

---

28. "Wenig ermutigender Anfang der Leipziger Messe,"
Sueddeutsche Zeitung, September 3, 1984, p. 17.

29. "VW-Motoren kuenftig auch aus der DDR?" Frankfurter
Allgemeine Zeitung, February 9, 1984, p. 1.

30. See "Frankreichs Premier in Ost-Berlin," Die Zeit,
June 21, 1985, p. 2.

following the construction of the wall cut ridership
substantially. The succeeding years brought deficits
that ranged from DM80 to 140 million annually and a very
embarrassing labor dispute. The GDR finally decided to
rid itself of this costly symbol. It found the city of
West Berlin to be a willing buyer (using federal money).

It is almost inconceivable that the GDR could now
cut itself off economically from the West. To the $1.25
billion per year in official FRG transfers must be added
the enormous flows from family gifts, travel, and border
fees. The West German mark has become a kind of second
currency in the GDR. The government tolerates an
expanded black market in part because it satisfies
public demand. Abandoning all this is now not simply
economically, but also politically, all but impossible.

West Berlin

West Berlin has welcomed its increased economic
interaction with the GDR. It is a spatial fact of life
that West Berlin must come to terms with the GDR for its
basic needs. Now it can move beyond the issues of electricity and garbage to more sophisticated and beneficial
areas of interdependence. The West Berlin government has
made no secret of its desire to operate more independently. Wilhelm Kewenig, West Berlin senator for science
and research, argued publicly in 1984 that Berlin should
be removed from the role of a simple object in Bonn's
Deutschlandpolitik. Kewenig called for greater flexibility and more opportunities for West Berlin's
interaction with the GDR on its own initiative.31/
West Berlin still faces formidable obstacles. On
the one hand, the GDR welcomes any opportunity to underscore its claim that the city is an independent
political entity. On the other hand, the GDR has no
desire to do anything to make West Berlin more affluent,
more viable, and more permanent. Yet the West Berlin
government seems undaunted. In order to manage better
the rapidly growing trade with the GDR, including the
frequent complex barter transactions that characterize
it, the city set up in November 1984 a Committee for
Trade with the GDR.

The Berlin Problem in a New Phase

Berlin has long suffered from its position at the

____

31. Joachim Nawrocki, "Berlinpolitik: Senat als Vor-
denker," Die Zeit, March 9, 1984, p. 5.

fulcrum of East-West conflict. The tension that continues to divide the Soviet bloc from NATO makes any prediction about the future of Berlin very difficult. Yet the signs of recent years are very positive for West Berlin and for its citizens.

First, there is good evidence that economic relations are now on firm enough ground that they have been largely decoupled from East-West issues. For example, the GDR asked the West German government for a DM1 billion credit at the height of the Soviet Union's anti-FRG missile deployment campaign. On the other side, the numerous spy scandals of 1985 had virtually no effect on the Federal Republic's willingness to continue vigorous economic relations.

Second, as the GDR agrees to more joint ventures and similar long-term commitments, it deepens its structural ties to the West. Thus far, at least, the Soviets are applauding these agreements. The new Soviet General Secretary Gorbachev praised the GDR's economic progress in 1985. The Soviets seem to be aware the GDR's ties to the FRG, vexing though they may be otherwise, provide the CMEA unique access to Western resources.

Finally, it is important to remember that none of these developments indicates a fundamental realignment of political goals. Still, there are nascent indications that West Berlin might be able to arrest its demographic and economic attrition. Berlin's leadership appears intent on pursuing all avenues for economic growth, including the GDR. Berlin is no longer content to remain a quiet dependent. Given the objective needs of the GDR, there is certainly potential for greater interaction and even for political byproducts that improve the lot of Berliners on both sides of the wall.

10

Postwar Berlin: Divided City

Richard L. Merritt

Greater Berlin, one of the world's largest cities spatially and boasting almost 4,500,000 inhabitants in 1943, suffered three successive waves of disruption during the next half-decade that left its population staggered, divided, but far from broken.

The first disruptive wave came with aerial bombardments and, in April 1945 when the Red Army stormed the city, savage streetfighting. It reduced greater parts of the city to piles of rubble. The U.S. Strategic Bombing Survey, for instance, estimated that 42 percent of Berlin's 1.5 million dwelling units were completely destroyed, and another 31 percent damaged to a lesser or greater extent; German sources estimated that they removed 98 million cubic yards of rubble from the city.1/ Evacuations reduced its population by a third from the peak of 1943. The destruction also crippled Berlin's communications and transportation facilities no less than its capacity to provide such normal municipal services as electricity, gas, water, and sewage removal.

The bombing and streetfighting nonetheless had a random effect as far as the eastern and western halves of the city were concerned. East Berlin, that is, the Soviet-occupied sector, lost 24 percent of its population and 23 percent of its industrial capacity, the three western sectors 27 percent of their population and 24 percent of their industrial capacity. East Berlin, with 37 percent of Berlin's dwelling units, accounted for 26 percent of the bombing losses and 40 percent of

---

1. Peter Paul Nahm, ed., <u>Dokumente deutscher Kriegsschaeden</u>, vol. IV/2: <u>Berlin--Kriegs- und Nachkriegsschicksal der Reichshauptstadt</u> (Bonn: Bundesministerium fuer Vertriebene, Fluechtlinge und Kreigsgeschaedigte, 1967), pp. 5-6, 74-77.

154

the rubble.2/

     The effects of the second disruptive wave were
distributed less equitably. Berlin fell to the Red Army
on May 2, 1945, but not until July 1 did the Western
Allies take over their occupation sectors in the city.
During these two months Soviet occupation authorities
extensively dismantled the city's remaining industrial
capacity to ship off to the USSR as reparations.3/
Possibly because of the unsettled nature of the reparations agreements, possibly because of the critical
importance to the Soviet Union of western Berlin's
industry, possibly (as Western writers have charged)
because of the realization that the Red Army would
eventually have to yield the western sectors to U.S.,
British, and French contingents, possibly (as Eastern
writers have explained) because of concern that the West
would fail to live up to the wartime Allies' tacit
agreements on reparations--whatever the cause, the
effect was that dismantling during these two months cost
West Berlin twice as much of its total industrial
capacity (with the loss estimated variously at between
53 and 67 percent) as East Berlin had suffered (25-33
percent).4/

     The third disruptive wave constituted the division
of the city itself. Soon after Berlin's joint occupation by the four Powers, cooperation broke down along
east-west lines.5/ The underlying issues were global in

---

2. Ibid., pp. 82-83; Statistisches Landesamt Berlin,
Berlin in Zahlen 1951 (Berlin [West]: Kulturbuch-Ver-
lag, 1951), p. 15.

3. The enemies of Hitler's Third Reich had never really
reached a final agreement on repartations. At Yalta the
Big Three had agreed in principle on the demand for
reparations, and specific sums, such as Stalin's pro-
posal of $20 billion, had been bandied about; postwar
agreements even specified how transfers were to be made.
But, in the final analysis, behavior regarding reparations was decentralized, with each occupying Power pursuing somewhat different policies in its own zone. See
Bruce Kuklick, American Policy and the Division of Germany: The Clash with Russia over Reparations (Ithaca,
N.Y.: Cornell University Press, 1972).

4. Nahm, Dokumente, vol. IV/2: Berlin, pp. 79-83.

5. See W. Phillips Davison, The Berlin Blockade: A
Study in Cold War Politics (Princeton, N.J.: Princeton
University Press, 1958); and Gerhard Keiderling and
Percy Stulz, Berlin 1945-1968: Zur Geschichte der
Hauptstadt der DDR und der selbstaendigen politischen

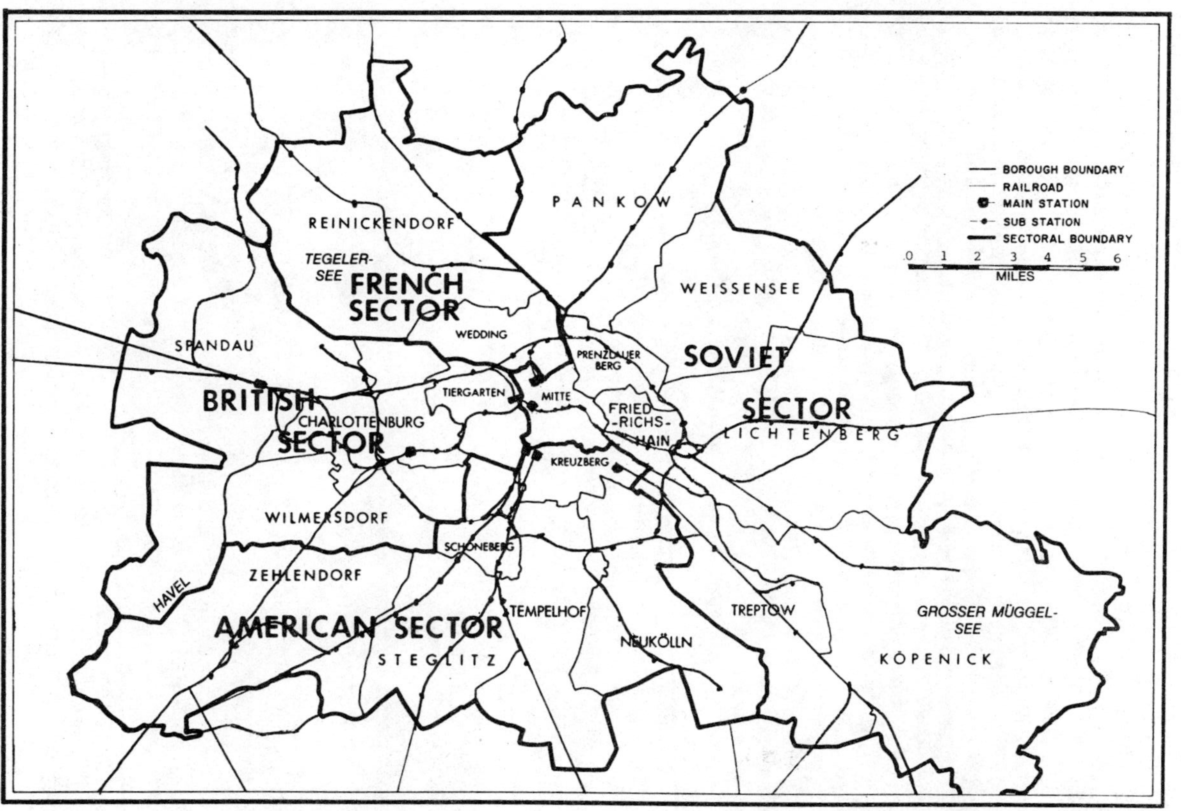

Figure 10.1:   Borough and Sectoral Boundaries of Greater Berlin, 1945

scope, but it was in Berlin that their practical effects were felt. These effects had to do with the provision of electricity and other municipal services; arrests and other forms of harassment; control over records and historical documents; and midnight confiscations of garbage cans, trucks, and building material. By March 1948 the Four-power Kommandatura split. Three months later, after the Western currency reform and the Soviet currency reform in response, came the blockade of the western sectors of Berlin and the West's counterblockade of those areas of Germany and Berlin under Soviet control. The processes of quasi-unified municipal government broke down in August 1948, to be replaced by separate governments in East and West Berlin. A Soviet-American agreement in May 1949 ended the blockade and counterblockade. It failed, however, to resolve the underlying issues spawned by the cold war, and left Berlin a divided city.

The question I shall address is how Berliners and their governments learned to cope with their divided city. The focus will be less on high-level diplomacy and intergovernmental relations than on the people living in the city. After all, whether or not a population learns to consider itself a single political community--sharing major values, responding to each other's concerns, identifying with one another, and all the rest--and whether or not the members of a formerly unified political community learn to accept its division into separate political communities depend less on official decrees than on the sentiments and behaviors of human beings carrying out their everyday lives. After surveying the political development of Berlin since 1945, I shall look at infrastructural, organizational, and behavioral changes in the city before turning to the question of the future of divided Berlin.

BERLIN IN THE VORTEX OF WORLD POLITICS

The political division of Berlin was a direct consequence of the breakdown of the anti-Axis alliance of World War II. The architects of peace during the wartime period had had a daring vision: that any resolution of the global problem of peace would necessarily rely on full cooperation between East and West. They were at best reluctant to plan for the eventuality that this cooperation would collapse. When the reality of conflict replaced the vision of cooperation, many unanticipated issues rose to the surface--not the least of which was the anomaly of Western troops in charge of

---

Einheit West Berlin (Berlin [East]: Dietz Verlag, 1970).

part of a city lying deep inside the Soviet zone of occupation without guaranteed rights of overland access.

The political division brought by the blockade was no doubt not the Soviet goal when its troops stopped all highway, railroad, and canal traffic between the western sectors of Berlin and western zones of Germany. The Soviet Union evidently expected that this pressure would force the West to relinquish its hold on the island-city. The West responded instead by setting up an airlift that could provision both the occupying forces and the two and a quarter million West Berliners in their charge. Faced by the success of the airlift, the Soviets then tried to take over the city's government. Massive efforts to intimidate West Berlin's representatives, who comprised a strong majority of the assembly, forced them to remove their offices to the American sector, where they set up shop again. Meanwhile, those remaining in the East quickly reorganized and, in November 1949, proclaimed a new government. Berlin thus had two governments, each proclaiming jurisdiction over the entire city but each in fact limited to areas controlled by its protective occupation forces.

What ensued was close to a dozen years during which the status of Berlin was cloudy. On the one hand, the governments in East and West Berlin acted increasingly independently of each other in a formal sense; and, by the mid-1950s, even the broad range of unofficial contacts which had continued were broken off. Officials in the West indicated that what they knew about the actions of their counterparts in the East came almost exclusively from newspaper reports. The principle of Four-power occupation, on the other hand, remained intact, and with it the notion that, legally at least, Berlin remained a single city. There was relatively free mobility across the line separating the two halves of the city. A small number of people even lived in one half while working in the other. Then, too, the citizens of neither were granted full rights of participation in the national parliaments created in the Federal Republic of Germany (FRG) in the West and the German Democratic Republic (GDR) in the East.

The GDR's decision in August 1961 to build a wall around West Berlin radically transformed the city's political context and expectations. Viewed from the perspective of Walter Ulbricht and his colleagues in the East German government, the step was certainly understandable. The open border in Berlin since 1949 had contributed significantly to the flight of over three million GDR citizens--about a sixth of its total population, over half of them young men just entering the labor market, and including very large numbers of doctors, engineers, and other trained technicians. It had also provided East Germans with ready access to the glitter of West Berlin, to a very public display of what their life might be like were they not saddled with their communist system. By building the wall the GDR made clear its intention to stabilize the status quo. It dashed any hopes that may have remained in East or West that Germany or Berlin would be reunited in the near future.

The tension caused by the wall, and it was intense during the first months after it was built, eventually gave way to a more moderate attitude that legitimized the new status quo. At the outset, of course, there was great cause for concern. Propagandistic fusillades were fired across the wall in both directions, and by October 1961 Soviet and American tanks faced each other a few meters apart at Checkpoint Charlie. As late as the following spring Soviet MIGs were still buzzing downtown West Berlin at dangerously low altitudes. The Cuban missile crisis of October 1962, however, brought mutual accommodations; and the simple passage of time accustomed people to the wall's existence even if they did not like it. By 1969 the political climate had changed to such an extent that West Germany's new Social Democratic chancellor, Willy Brandt, could initiate a policy of relaxation that ultimately included, among other things, a Four-power agreement on Berlin in 1971 and subsequent intra-German agreements that eased the lot of West Berliners and permitted them once again to cross the border into the East. Later moves by the GDR tied East Berlin ever closer to the political and constitutional structure of the German Democratic Republic.

Elaborate interpretations of its underlying meanings notwithstanding, the Quadripartite and other agreements of 1971-73 had the effect of giving the status quo of divided Berlin a seal of acceptance (albeit not, at least in Western eyes, approval). Thus it has remained in the years since then. But, while it may be a relatively simple matter to draw a political boundary and enforce it with immigration officers and, if necessary, bayonets and barbed wire, to divide a city and political community which act as an organic unity is quite a different matter.

INFRASTRUCTURAL DIVISION

The political boundary between East and West Berlin, while based on borough boundaries that had long existed, is artificial in every other sense. Spatially, for example, the development of Greater Berlin was not unlike that of most other metropolises of its time. It had a core area comprising the central business district, government buildings, and cultural institutions such as theaters and the university; an inner ring of densely populated apartment buildings and an outer ring of suburban growth; and an integrated network of

subway lines, sewers, water pipes, and the like that
served the city as a whole. The long-term success of
any political division not based on popular wishes would
necessarily rest upon the disruption of that integrated
infrastructure.

Municipal Services

     That change could not come overnight can be seen in
the example of Berlin's municipal utilities.6/ Geographic circumstances had played a role in the
reconstruction of these services following the wartime
damage and postwar dismantling. In contrast to the gas
and water companies, which had their main offices in the
western sectors, the electricity company was located in
the Soviet sector and, since the Red Army had shipped
off over 90 percent of the power-generating facilities
outside their own sector, the western sectors of the
city were almost totally reliant on decisions made in
the East. The sewage system, which interlaced the
entire city, poured about 98 percent of its raw sewage
into leeching fields and treatment centers located in
the Soviet sector or zone.
     The experience of the blockade made West Berliners
insist on complete independence from the East with
respect to most of these municipal services. During the
blockade months Soviet authorities had simply shut off
the flow of electricity to the western sectors,
presumably as a means of bringing pressure to bear upon
them. Even in the winter months of 1948-49 the average
household in West Berlin received only two hours of
electricity per day--and then at sometimes unpredictable
hours. The Western Allies responded by flying into the
city whole generators, part by part, to rebuild the
Western Power Plant dismantled by the Soviets; and
provided economic assistance after the blockade to spur
the development of West Berlin's power-generating
capacity. By early 1955 West Berlin produced all its
own electricity.
     Separation, wherever it was feasible, became the
rule for the other utilities as well. This process was
completed for the gas company by 1950 and for the water-
works a decade later. West Berlin aimed at independence
in rubbish disposal by constructing enormous incinera-
tors. The increase in rubbish that accompanies
prosperity, however, outstripped the increase in

---

6. See my "Political Division and Municipal Services in
Postwar Berlin," in Public Policy 17, eds. John D.
Montgomery and Albert O. Hirschmann (Cambridge, Mass.:
Harvard University Press, 1968).

capacities to handle it, with the consequence that West Berlin ultimately had to negotiate with the GDR to dispose of it effectively. The city also continues to pay the GDR substantial sums every year to accept its untreated sewage (which the GDR, in turn, uses for fertilizing and other profitable purposes); both sides realize that a disruption of this service would produce unwanted consequences, such as the pollution of waterways flowing through Berlin and the GDR.

Spatial Organization

Buildings and streets, we might think, are even more resistant to change dictated by political circumstances than are municipal utilities.7/ An examination of spatial developments in Berlin since the war nevertheless reveals that political demands, at least when implemented unrelentingly, can have a significant impact in these regards as well.

Not the least of these developments stemmed from West Berlin's loss of the core area functions it shared with the eastern sector when Greater Berlin was still Germany's capital city. The division of Germany into separate and mutually antagonistic countries, West Berlin's exposed location deep inside the GDR, and the ever present possibility of yet another blockade conspired to push West Berlin to the periphery of West German life. Bonn took over the function of political capital, Hamburg became the center of commerce, and Frankfurt is the FRG's financial center. Nor do the country's major cultural impulses come almost exclusively from Berlin anymore, as was true in the 1920s. By contrast, the East German leadership, perhaps unwisely from some perspectives, chose to build up "Democratic Berlin" as the country's capital and locate there its main core area functions.

What is happening is a process of adjustment: West Berlin is reducing the scope of its political and economic activity to bring it into balance with its current capabilities. In the short run this process can turn West Berlin into a self-sufficient, viable political entity, besides making life in the city even more pleasantly bearable. Its long-run effect, however, is to reinforce the consequences of the city's division: the encapsulation and withdrawal of West Berlin from its traditional hinterland, and the acceptance by West Berlin of a peripheral position in West German life, in

---

7. See my "Infrastructural Changes in Berlin," Annals of the Association of American Geographers 63:1 (March 1973): 58-70.

contrast to the centrality enjoyed by Greater Berlin before 1945 and by East Berlin in the German Democratic Republic today.

Just as Greater Berlin was the core area for prewar Germany, so too the borough of Mitte, or City Center, was the heart of Berlin. It contained the Reich's most important administrative offices, the city hall, and key embassies. Streets such as Unter den Linden and monuments such as the Brandenburg Gate were known to the world. Mitte had the university, state library, world-famous museums, state opera, cathedral, national theater, and a host of other cultural establishments. It was the center of Germany's newspaper and book trade. Two thirds of Berlin's insurance firms, three quarters of its banks, and half of its ladies' garment manufacturers were located within a few blocks of each other. Mitte, no more than 4.1 square miles in size, clearly set prewar Germany's political, economic, and cultural patterns.

The political division of 1948 sharply reduced Mitte's practical importance and even symbolic value. Wartime destruction, of course, had all but wiped out Mitte. After the fighting stopped and the occupation began, however, it once again became the focal point of Berlin life--under the aegis of the Soviet Union, in whose sector of occupation it lay. The city hall and other municipal offices began operations, often in provisional quarters, to be sure, and eventually theaters, the university, and the opera opened their doors again. The borough was prepared to resume its rightful role as core area of one of the world's largest cities.

With the split came the realization for West Berliners that they would have to look elsewhere for a core area, at least until the city should be reunified. Least problematic was the search for a new central business district. Even before the war writers and statisticians had noticed certain movements away from Mitte. The most important was the emergence of a fashionable shopping center near the Berlin zoo and the Kaiser Wilhelm Memorial Church in the borough of Char-lottenburg, about two miles southwest of the Brandenburg Gate. The availability of less-damaged buildings had led to a small-scale revival before the blockade; political division and the economic recovery of West Berlin in the ensuing years merely enhanced this trend.

Before the 1950s were over the Zoo Quarter had firmly established itself as West Berlin's new core area (Figure 10.2). It housed the major businesses and the stock exchange. With its leading restaurants, first-run movie houses, and exclusive shops it became the focal point of tourists and West Berliners alike. Traffic patterns which had once had Mitte as their nodal point now had the Zoo Quarter. Gradually, too, government

Figure 10.2:
Shift of Berlin's central business district, 1945-1985

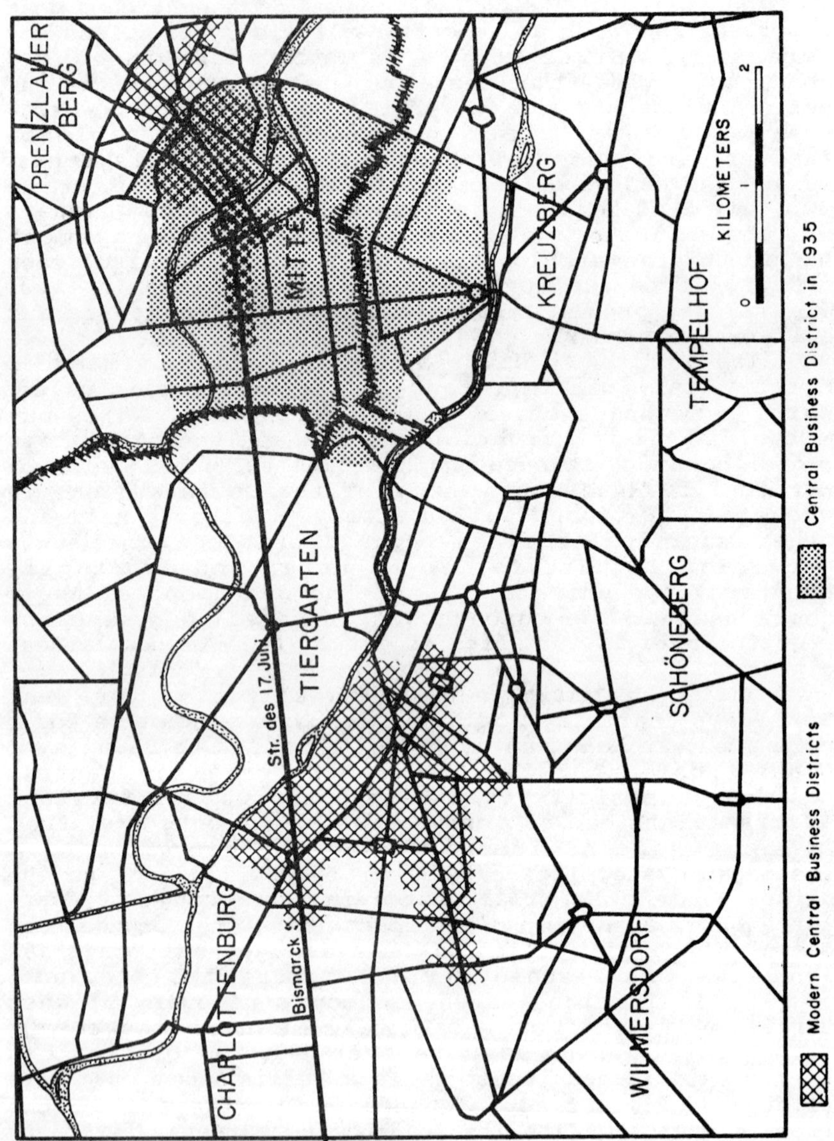

offices drifted from their temporary quarters to a belt just to the south of this core area; and residential patterns began to accommodate themselves to the changing structure of West Berlin. In many ways, the brightly-lit Kurfuerstendamm, which runs through the center of the Zoo Quarter, has come to symbolize postwar Berlin in the popular mind just as the magnificent Unter den Linden did for old Berlin.

Meanwhile, East Berlin's core area was moving eastwards. Rebuilding in the immediate postwar period had concentrated on buildings in the western half of Mitte, not far from the intersection of Unter den Linden and Friedrichstrasse and fairly close to the West Berlin boroughs of Tiergarten and Kreuzberg. After 1949 city planners began to rebuild residential areas in the inner boroughs of Prenzlauer Berg and Friedrichshain (including a gigantic residential and shopping complex on the latter's main artery, then Stalinallee but since 1961 Karl Marx Allee). The politburo of the communist party's central committee decided in September 1964 to focus new construction around Alexander Square, 1.7 miles east of the Brandenburg Gate and near the point where the boroughs of Mitte, Prenzlauer Berg, and Friedrichshain meet. Since then, "Alex," as Berliners fondly term it, has become to East Berlin what the Zoo Quarter is to West Berlin.

The infrastructural aspects of a political community, as suggested earlier, exhibit remarkable durability and tenacity in resisting change. The very tenacity of the infrastructure, however, suggests that, once change is initiated, its reversal will be very difficult. The developments briefly summarized here thus portend an ever growing divergence of West and East Berlin, respectively, from the old center of Greater Berlin, and increased solidification of each around its own new core area.

ORGANIZATIONAL DIVISION

To some measure people organize their lives around the voluntary associations in which they participate. Accordingly, if we would fully understand people's perspectives and behaviors, we must look at their organizational ties. The division of Germany and Berlin in 1948-49 forced most associations previously unified across the new boundaries to follow suit. Even informal interaction among the branches in East and West became subject to political considerations. In Berlin, for example, politicization went so far that the East German regime forbade intracity athletic competition. Such pressures notwithstanding, three voluntary associations of major political significance sought to retain intact their organizational structure across the territories of

164

the two Berlins: the Social Democratic party and the Protestant and Catholic churches.

Social Democracy

Politics in Berlin has long leaned to the left.8/ Although neither the home of the party itself nor the birthplace of its early leaders, imperial Berlin was the arena in which the Social Democratic Party of Germany (SPD) came to national prominence; and it is quite understandable that Social Democrats anticipated regaining political power in the city once Nazism had been defeated. Indeed, they were well on their way to doing so, and in the process all but eclipsing the communist party (KPD), when in April 1946 the Soviets engineered in the territories they controlled a merger of the two parties into the Socialist Unity party (SED). The Four-power status of Berlin nonetheless gave both parties, the SPD and the SED, the right to operate freely throughout the entire city.

Freedom in principle, though, did not mean freedom in practice. For the SPD-East to have participated fully in the political process in East Berlin would have meant subordinating itself and its principles to the all-encompassing, SED-dominated National Front. The party's leaders would rather have dissolved the SPD-East than agree to such a proposition. They thus assumed the role of symbolic rather than active opposition to the SED's regime. Joining the party was not a way to influence the course of political events. It meant taking a stance that rejected the entire East German political system.

Not surprisingly, the SPD-East atrophied. Young people were reluctant to associate with it; and many of all ages who were members withdrew in the face of police harassment or else fled to the West. The membership roster, with approximately 25,000 dues-paying members in March 1946, declined to 8,330 in December 1950 and to 5,327 in June 1961, six weeks before the wall went up.9/ Those who remained became increasingly isolated. The

---

8. See my "The SPD of East Berlin, 1945-1961" (with Ronald A. Francisco), Comparative Politics 5:1 (October 1972): 1-28.

9. Estimated data for 1946 are from Albrecht Kaden, Einheit oder Freiheit: Die Wiedergruendung der SPD 1945-1946 (Hanover: Verlag J.A.W. Dietz Nachf. Gmbh, 1964), p. 320n; data for 1950 and 1961 are from Sozialdemokratische Partei Deutschlands, Landesverband Berlin, Jahresbericht, volumes for 1951 and 1962 (mimeographed).

party itself evolved from an open parliamentary system into a closed group with conspiratorial aspects. Finally, in August 1961, realizing that the construction of the wall had rendered the SPD-East untenable, the parent body in West Berlin dissolved it.

Churches

The place of organized religion in Berlin after 1945 presents a more complex picture. In the case of the more numerous Protestants, the territorial basis of their provincial church reached back into the sixteenth century for its origin. Greater Berlin was but one of four dioceses comprising the Evangelical Church in Berlin-Brandenburg (EKBB), which had its seat in the western borough of Charlottenburg. The other three dioceses were in the Soviet zone of occupation. What is more, its first postwar bishop, Otto Dibelius, also chaired the council of the federation of Germany's 28 provincial churches, the Evangelical Church in Germany (EKD), created in July 1948. The Catholic diocese, too, extended beyond Berlin's borders to include a substantial portion of what is now the German Democratic Republic.

With the division of Germany and Berlin came pressure from the GDR, which was not friendly to religion in the first place, to make state boundaries those of the churches as well. Both the EKD and EKBB resisted this pressure. Church leaders argued that no state had the right to mix into the church's internal affairs, including its organizational framework. Some, such as Bishop Dibelius, even questioned the very legitimacy of the East German regime, and seemed to be pushing East German Protestantism into the kind of underground battle against that regime that many Protestant leaders had conducted against Hitler's totalitarianism.10/ The effect was to hamper churches in East Germany and East Berlin in both their organizational tasks and their efforts to take Christianity to the individual.

Eventually the Protestants had to make concessions to the East German state. In 1969 the country's eight provincial churches formally broke off from the EKD to form a League of Evangelical Churches in the German Democratic Republic (BEK). Symbolic unity was nonetheless retained. The BEK's constitution not only committed the League to be part of a "special community"

____

10. See his letter to Bishop Hans Lilje, <u>Obrigkeit: Eine Frage an den 60jaehrigen Landesbischof</u> (Berlin [West]: n.p., 1959).

comprising the "whole of Evangelical Christianity in Germany," it went on to assert the BEK's preparedness, "in the freedom born of partnership," to act accordingly on "issues which affect in common all Evangelical churches in the German Democratic Republic and in the Federal Republic of Germany." The EKBB struggled against division until the end of 1972. At that time, instead of formally breaking up its organizational structure, provincial church leaders in both East and West agreed to the establishment of a second bishopric to be responsible for the dioceses in East Berlin and Brandenburg, and adopted language that permitted each region to act as autonomously as was required. Since then, widespread cooperation and coordination have characterized the relationship between the two bishoprics in Berlin-Brandenburg as well as that between the EKD and BEK.

The Catholic Church's willingness to make needed adjustments early gave it substantially more breathing room to develop its response to the state. Even before the wall went up the church had made plans to install an East Berliner as bishop (although he was not enthroned until afterwards); and six years later Bishop Alfred Bengsch wore a cardinal's hat. At a time when other East Berliners were not permitted to go to the West, Bishop Bengsch was free to visit his parishioners in West Berlin.11/ This _modus vivendi_ is challenged from time to time, of course, but more to secure specific concessions than to open up the question of splitting West Berlin off from the Berlin bishopric.

What is less clear than the tactics pursued by the churches is the impact that their organizational structure had on members of their congregations. The impression obtained from interviews with Protestant officials in West Berlin is that most citizens who consider themselves religious are more concerned with personal than structural matters, and have a rather abstract notion of what the actual relationship between the churches in East and West actually is. The pastor of a parish split in 1961 by the wall, a parish that was once quite active in maintaining contacts with its sister church on the other side, notes that his parishioners nowadays are paying attention to other things, such as assistance to developing countries and nuclear disarmament. A quantitative analysis of the

---

11. In 1967, at the time Bishop Bengsch was named cardinal, there were 505,000 Catholics in the Berlin bishopric: 256,000 in West Berlin, 110,000 in East Berlin, and 139,000 in the GDR. Data from "Pabst Paul ernannte 27 neue Kardinaele," _Der Tagesspiegel_ (Berlin [West]), May 30, 1967, p. 2.

distribution of news in the EKBB's weekly newspaper, <u>Die Kirche</u>, bears out this impression. News from parishes in East Berlin has virtually disappeared from its columns.

Insisting on formal structural unity within Berlin's churches ultimately served the same purposes as keeping the SPD as a functioning body throughout the city. Both performed the symbolic function of defiance. They demonstrated to the East German regime that some groups would not buckle before its political demands; and provided a beacon light of hope to individual citizens who needed to know that they were not alone in opposing that regime. Both also supported those whom the regime had crushed or was placing under pressure. At the level of the individual prepared to be a Christian in a socialist state, however, or wanting to exert political influence in society, the value of such functions soon wore thin. Then, too, younger generations who grew up in a divided city have been less than impressed by the causes that inspired their elders. The task for most people is learning to live with the status quo, not changing it.

BEHAVIORAL SEPARATION

Well, then, what about the Berliners? How did they respond to the measures aimed at tearing apart the political community they had shared? Various kinds of public opinion data, although not specific to this theme, strongly suggest that most Berliners would favor the reunification of their city, but are aware that the prospects for this outcome are dim in the near future. But political community rests on more than sentimental attachments. It also depends on people behaving in a fashion consistent with those sentiments. This raises the question, Have Berliners utilized the opportunities available to them after 1949 to maintain contacts with the other side of the city. In the absence of data on the behavior of individuals as such, data which either do not exist or have not been made publicly available, we must rely on indicators of behavior at the aggregate level to answer such a question.

The results of such a survey are discouraging as far as the maintenance of ties between East and West Berlin is concerned. Even after the division of 1948, for instance, the border between the two parts of the city remained open, at least in principle. Citizens of one side merely had to board a subway or elevated railway to get to the other side, or else simply walk across at any of 86 border stations. Any risk that such a step entailed remained fairly constant from the end of the blockade in 1949 to the construction twelve years later of a wall that ended virtually all Berliners' travel to the other side of their city. Yet indicators based on a wide variety of interpersonal transactions--Eastern visitors to the theater and other events in West Berlin, letters and packages sent between West Berlin and the East, subscriptions to a West Berlin newspaper held by Easterners, and the like--all dropped markedly between 1949 and 1961.12/ A composite index summarizing these indicators (Figure 10.3) suggests that the rate of declining contacts was greatest at the outset of the 1950s and then, by about 1958, flattened out considerably.

If the 1950s, years in which the border between East and West Berlin was relatively open, were an era of declining interaction, what would the closing of that border in 1961 bring? We might expect--and East German authorities doubtless hoped--that virtually complete separation would whittle down the last vestiges of community. Alternatively, given the strong West German emphasis on maintaining contacts with relatives and friends "over there," we might expect a surge in the forms of interaction that remained possible.

The reality, as indicated by available data, conformed completely to neither expectation.13/ Opportunities for interpersonal contacts between East and West Berliners were few and far between. In the mid-1960s, when visits to East Berlin during holiday periods were permitted, a substantial number of West Berliners obtained entry passes. The number of permits ranged from approximately one for every two Berliners during the Christmas and New Year's holidays in 1963-64--the first opening in the wall after August 1961--to less than half that number during the Easter and Whitsuntide holidays in 1966. Insofar as such a brief time period

---

12. See my "Political Disintegration in Postwar Berlin," in From National Development to Global Community: Essays in Honor of Karl W. Deutsch, eds. Richard L. Merritt and Bruce M. Russett (London: George Allen and Unwin, 1981). The indicators surveyed (and summarized in the composite index) are: Eastern visitors to West Berlin's municipal theaters, exhibition center, radio tower, and summer garden, 1950-1961; letters and packages sent between West Berlin and the East, 1952-1960; membership in the SPD-East, 1950-1961; and sales of the daily newspaper Telegraf to East Berlin subscribers, 1951-1960.

13. Data in this and the following paragraphs are from my "Interpersonal Transactions across the Wall," in Living with the Wall: West Berlin, 1961-1985, eds. Richard L. Merritt and Anna J. Merritt (Durham, N.C.: Duke University Press, 1985), pp. 166-183.

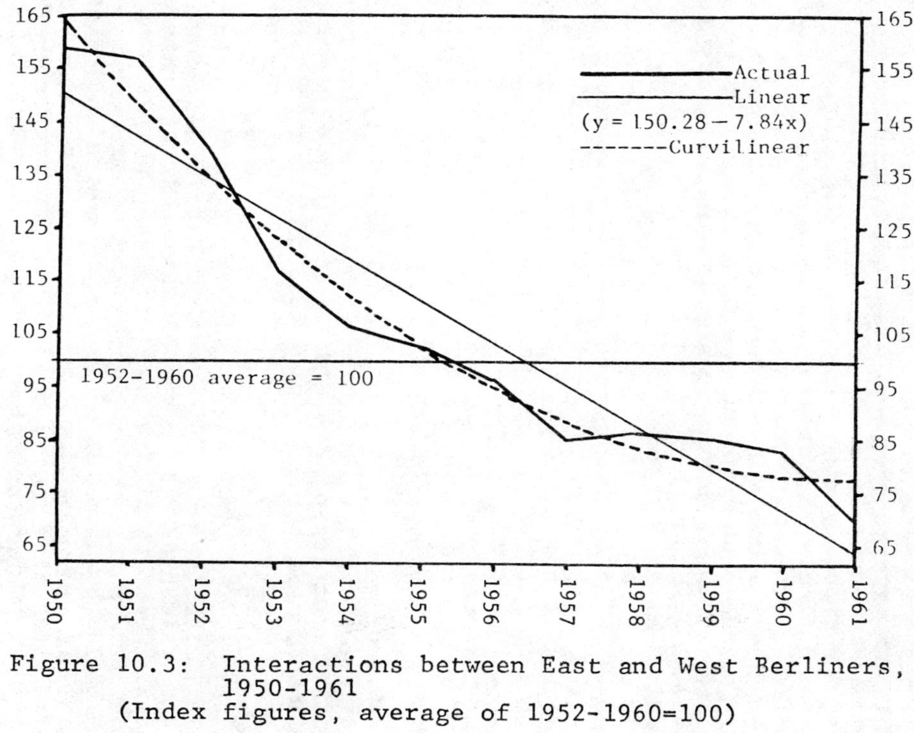

Figure 10.3: Interactions between East and West Berliners, 1950-1961
(Index figures, average of 1952-1960=100)

reveals trends in interpersonal contacts, they were downward. The distribution of emergency visiting permits because of pressing family matters also hints at a declining trend even though, as the East German authorities discovered that such traffic was financially profitable, the criteria for giving them to West Berliners were liberalized. The number of packages shipped to or received from the East as well as attention patterns in West Berlin's weekly Protestant newspaper strengthen the impression that the trend of declining interest in the East among West Berliners was real and not the artifact of any particular analytic approach.

The Quadripartite Agreement of September 1971 laid the groundwork for at least a partial opening of the borders. Later that year the West Berlin Senate and the GDR agreed, among other things, to permit West Berliners to visit East Berlin and the GDR for up to 30 days per year (even more in some cases, such as illness in the family), and create offices in West Berlin to process applications. Although the traffic would be for the most part one-way, that is, for West Berliners only, the prospects nevertheless existed to re-establish ties severed or weakened during the 1960s. The significant question is how these West Berliners actually responded to the opportunity to reassert their sense of community across the wall.

Figures on the actual number of visits West Berliners made to the East are striking in a couple of respects. First, the number of visits per year declined over the last dozen years, from 3.72 million from June 4, 1972 to May 31, 1973 to 1.56 million between June 1, 1981 and May 31, 1984 (Figure 10.4). A linear regression characterizing the shifts in year-to-year figures indicates that the average number of visits declined by 177,600 per year. (If this trend were to continue unabated into the future, then by 1994 no West Berliners would be crossing the border!) Second, there are remarkable dips in the curve during 1973-75 and then again in 1980-82. In part this is due to the extraordinarily high figure for 1972-73, when people may have been rushing to take advantage of the agreement before it should be cancelled or to visit friends and relatives they may have not seen since 1966. In larger part, though, the dips coincide with the periods in which the GDR both raised the amount of hard currency which any visitor to the East was obligated to exchange and also expanded the number of individuals affected by the regulations. Visits lasting more than a single day seem to be less affected by the changes in fees than are those of shorter duration.

In a sense, the use of telephones may be replacing the mails as the chief means of communication between East and West Berliners. Packages shipped to the East

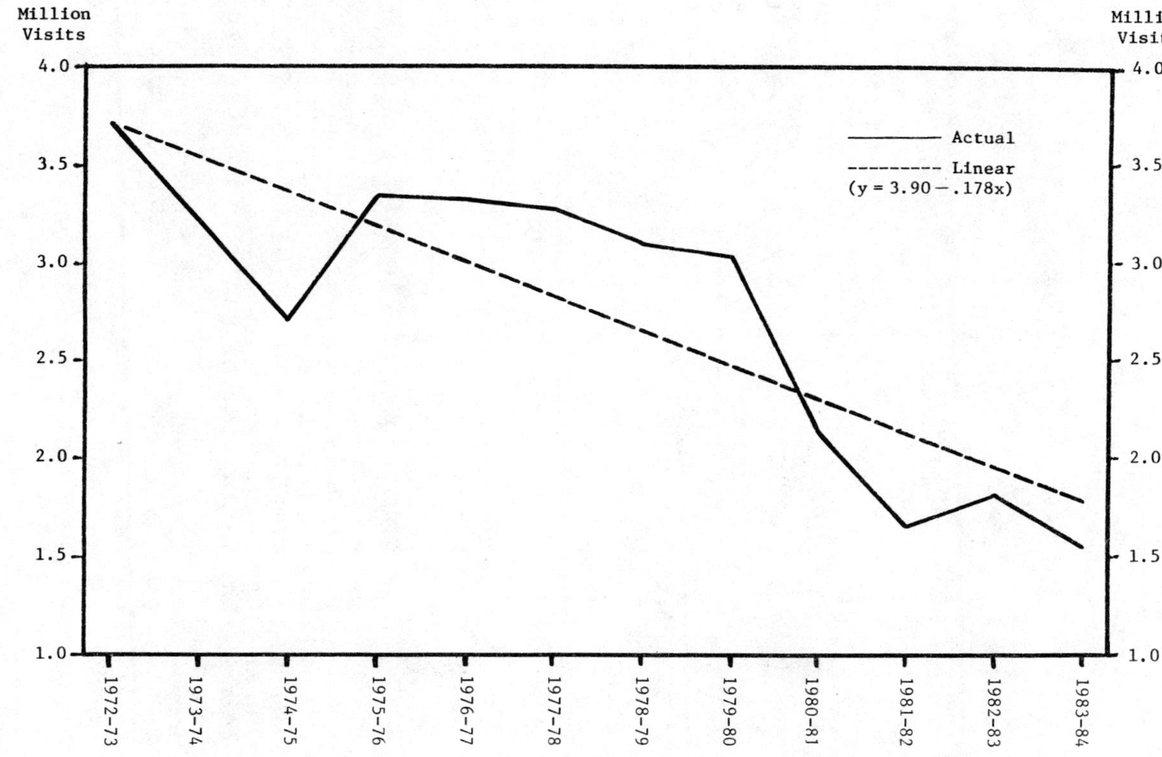

Figure 10.4: Number of visits by West Berliners to East Berlin and the GDR, 1972-84

continued to decline in the 1970s--from 7.41 million in 1971 to about two fifths that number (3.18 million) in 1977. As a result of the agreements of 1971-73, telephone service between the two halves of the city, broken off in the early 1950s, was restored, and the number of available lines was increased from year to year (from 40 in October 1971 to 609 in December 1981). In 1972-73 the daily traffic was roughly 8,200 calls to East Berlin; by 1981 the figure was 23,849 (down from 25,787 in the previous year).14/ The importance of these telephone calls as a means of sustaining a sense of community nonetheless remains to be seen. Not until a sufficient number of lines has been available for some time to handle desired conversations will it be possible to assess any trend. The most reasonable prediction to make is that, when ample lines are available for all who wish to telephone between East and West Berlin (and quite possibly before then, if the decline from 1980 to 1981 is a valid indicator), the number of calls actually made will begin to diminish.

The partial reopening of the border in 1971 thus has not reversed the longstanding drop-off of interpersonal ties between East and West Berliners. With the exception of telephone traffic, where we may already have seen a peaking, every indicator available for the past three decades--for the 1950s when the border was fully open, for the 1960s when it was closed, and for the 1970s when it was partially open again--shows a pattern of decreasing communication. East and West Berliners are increasingly leading lives that are separate from each other.

FUTURE OF DIVIDED BERLIN

The evidence summarized here on the infrastructural basis of Berlin's political community, the organizations that sought to retain their unity across the border, and the actual behavior of people in interacting with Berliners from the other side of the city points fairly consistently to a single conclusion: the decline of political community in postwar Berlin. Where once there was a single city, now there are two. And, in concrete terms, the two cities have precious little to do with each other.

----

14. Data from "Bericht ueber die Durchfuerung des Vier-Maechte-Abkommens und der ergaenzenden Vereinbarungen zwischen dem 3. Juni 1972 und dem 31. Mai 1973," Abgeordnetenhaus von Berlin, 6. Wahlperiode, Drucksache 6/1013, August 1, 1973, p. 7; and subsequent reports.

All this does not necessarily mean that political community is dead in Berlin. In this regard several facts are important to note. First, although the level of contacts is declining, the contacts have not disappeared. It is likely that most of the decline is attributable to superficial ties, such as tourism or visits to casual acquaintances, and that it will continue until only the firmest of familial ties or those of friendship continue to exist. In addition, there are signs that younger Berliners are interested in setting up new contacts with their age-cohorts on the other side of the city or in the GDR. Although such contacts are likely to be of the sort that exist between the youth (and other groups) in any two neighboring countries whose residents speak a common language, it is also possible that such relationships can add substantially to the bedrock of sentimental community.

Second, we would be unwise to dismiss out of hand the significance of the linkages that remain. That they have a political impact can be inferred from the decision of the GDR in summer 1980 to raise once again the financial costs for West Berliners and others crossing the border into the East. The East German regime, while encouraging tourism, wants to keep interpersonal contacts to a minimum. Each personal visit by a Westerner reminds its citizens once again that life could be different from what it is, that at the very least they would like to have the right to travel across the border.

Third, the forms of less personal interaction that exist have effects that no government can control completely. Writers from the two sides of the wall, for example, meet from time to time, discover that they have deepseated mutual interests, and go home to write articles and novels reflecting this perspective. Fragmentary evidence strongly suggests that the two thirds of the GDR population able to receive Western television in their homes are avid viewers, especially of news programs. Consultations among Protestant leaders in East and West paved the way for the decision made by many East German pastors to support a peace movement aimed at disarmament in their own part of the world. Readers of contemporary literature, television viewers, churchgoers, and many others are not insensitive to the message being sent out: "We Germans," it is saying, "have significant interests in common that go beyond our current commitment to mutually antagonistic military blocs. We belong together!"

Finally, it is possible albeit not very likely that major political breakthroughs will reunite the city and reverse the trend of declining community. This possibility of reversibility raises an interesting question: What would happen if Berlin were to be reunified today, or next week? Would not the old patterns of interaction, and with them the expectations, demands, and identifications associated with political community, simply re-emerge? In other words, have three decades and more of separation <u>really</u> made East and West Berliners different from each other?

In seeking to answer this question, it is tempting to think in terms of historical examples. Poles did not give up their sense of nationality despite a century and a quarter of division under alien rule; and similar nationality struggles were recurrent in the Balkans. Such examples, however, which would lead us to expect a sense of German nationality and Berlin community to persist for many decades to come, may be misleading. The classic cases of reunited nationalities occurred at times and in places in which there was a relatively low degree of organized complexity. Polish peasants in what were then the German, Russian, and Austro-Hungarian empires were fairly similar, more tied to the land and their peasant communities than to elaborate sets of imperial social communications systems. It is by no means clear that the Poland that re-emerged in 1918 was the result of spontaneous pressure from the masses, as opposed to an unusual set of international circum-stances, effective organization by a small number of leaders, and the willingness of the masses to cast votes in plebiscites. How likely is it that a new inter-national crisis would make the rest of the world accept a reunified Germany and/or Berlin? Moreover, although another element in the Polish case, a unifying thrust by determined leaders, may eventually exist in the German situation, what they will face is not a mass of peasants untied to any large-scale and complex system of government and communication, but rather populations with strong sets of interdependencies which are mutually exclusive.

The latter is a more likely scenario for a Berlin reunified at some future time. If the city is pol-itically amalgamated on the basis of new international agreements, it will be fairly easy to rebuild a unified municipal government, and with time it will be possible to construct the links to tie together divided water and electricity grids, streets and subway lines, and the like. Still more difficult to reconstruct will be the sentimental ties of community. Reunification in the year, say, 2000 will come more than a half century after the city's political division and almost 40 years after the appearance of the wall. By then there will be very few Berliners alive who will have a vivid memory of what it was like before 1945, and fewer still who will have any active contacts on the other side of the city. Changing residential preferences, traffic, and other patterns by which people organize their daily lives will by then have produced two cities in a physical sense. East Berliners will be tied intimately to the social, economic, political, and other systems in the German Democratic Republic; West Berliners to quite different systems in the Federal Republic. Rebuilding a common set of expectations, demands, and identifications among Berliners will doubtless be a slow process, quite possibly slower than that which had forced them apart in the first place. Even then, as the history of efforts to merge American towns and cities into larger units suggests, unforeseen issues may arise to hinder reunification.

What seems far less likely in the present circumstances is that a new nationalistic movement firmly grounded at the grassroots level will emerge to force the German governments or those of the victorious Allies of World War II to reunify the country (or, still less likely, Berlin alone). The precondition for such a movement would be the kind of social communications networks which the GDR's government still seems determined to prevent. Free mobility within Berlin and Germany will probably remain an impossible dream until there are no more economic incentives for citizens of one Germany to flee to the other, pacts have been reached for returning to their country of origin those who have left for political reasons (a possibility that most West German leaders would firmly reject now), and, more generally, neither country poses a threat to the other. It is unlikely that, in the absence of free mobility, an effective social communications network will emerge in the two Germanies.

The prospects, at least for the foreseeable future, are for the division of Berlin to continue. As each year passes, the underlying basis of political community in Berlin as a whole erodes a bit more. East Berliners become more closely tied to a network of systems that tries as much as possible to ignore the existence of West Berlin, while West Berliners form stronger links to a network of systems in which nongovernmental processes in East Berlin are of little moment. In the place of community, estrangement is growing.

Acronyms

BEK	League of Evangelical Churches in the GDR
CDU	Christian Democratic Union
CMEA	Council for Mutual Economic Assistance
CSCE	Conference on Security and Cooperation in Europe
CSU	Christian Social Union (Bavaria)
EAC	European Advisory Commission
EC	European Community
EEC	European Economic Community
EKBB	Evangelical Church in Berlin-Brandenburg
EKD	Evangelical Church in Germany
FRG	Federal Republic of Germany
GDR	German Democratic Republic
INF	Intermediate Nuclear Force
KPD	Communist Party of Germany
MBFR	Mutual and Balanced Force Reduction Talks
NVA	National People's Army (GDR)
SED	Socialist Unity Party of Germany
SEW	Socialist Unity Party of West Berlin
SPD	Social Democratic Party of Germany

About the Contributors

Caroline Bray is a research associate of the Policy Studies Institute, London.

Ronald A. Francisco is associate professor of political science and Soviet and East European studies at the University of Kansas.

Renata Fritsch-Bournazel is professor at the Fondation Nationales des Sciences Politiques, Paris.

William E. Griffith is Ford professor of political science at the Massachusetts Institute of Technology.

Roger Morgan is the head of the European Centre for Political Studies in the Policy Studies Institute, London.

Richard L. Merritt is professor of political science and research professor in communications, University of Illinois at Urbana-Champaign.

Edwina Moreton is a Soviet and East European specialist at The Economist (London).

Eberhard Schulz is deputy director of research, German Institute for Foreign Policy, Bonn.

Michael J. Sodaro is associate professor of international affairs and political science at the Institute for Sino-Soviet Studies, George Washington University.

Shepard Stone is director of the Aspen Institute, Berlin.

Gerhard Wettig specializes in Soviet and East European research at the Federal Institute for Eastern and International Studies, Cologne.

Index